Bank Secrecy Act/ Anti-Money Laundering Examination Manual for Money Services Businesses

2008

TABLE OF CONTENTS

INTRODUCTION

This *Bank Secrecy Act/Anti-Money Laundering Examination Manual for Money Services Businesses* provides guidance to examiners for performing Bank Secrecy Act (BSA) examinations.

As the administrator of the BSA, the Financial Crimes Enforcement Network (FinCEN) has delegated authority to the Internal Revenue Service (IRS) to examine the anti-money laundering (AML) program of money services businesses (MSBs). [1]

An effective AML program requires sound risk management; therefore, the manual also provides guidance on identifying and controlling risks associated with money laundering and terrorist financing. The manual contains an overview of AML program requirements, BSA/AML risks and risk management expectations, sound industry practices, and examination procedures. The development of this manual was a collaborative effort of the IRS, state agencies responsible for MSB regulation, the Money Transmitter Regulators Association (MTRA), the Conference of State Bank Supervisors (CSBS), and FinCEN, a bureau of the U.S. Department of the Treasury. The goal is to ensure consistency in the application of the BSA requirements.

The manual focuses on the following types of MSB activities[2]:

- Issuance, Sale, and Redemption of Money Orders;
- Issuance, Sale, and Redemption of Traveler's Checks;
- Money Transmission;
- Check Cashing; and
- Currency Exchange or Dealing.

---

1. 31 CFR 103. 56(b)(8) and 103.125(c). State regulators may also examine MSBs for compliance with certain BSA requirements, possibly including compliance with the AML program requirement, as elements of a more comprehensive list of compliance requirements imposed under state law. These requirements, however, will vary widely from state to state.

2. Under 31 CFR 103.11(uu) MSBs include each agent, agency, branch, or office within the United States doing business, whether or not on a regular basis or as an organized business concern, in one or more of the following capacities: (1) currency dealer or exchanger; (2) check casher; (3) issuers of traveler's checks, money orders or stored value; (4) sellers and redeemers of traveler's checks, money orders or stored value; (5) money transmitters; and (6) the U.S. Postal Service, except with respect to the sale of postage or philatelic products. A person offering a financial service specified in (1) through (4) above, who does not offer that service in an amount greater than $1,000 in currency or monetary or other instruments for any person on any day in one or more transactions is not included in the definition of MSB.

Objectives of Manual

The objectives of this manual are to:

- Provide guidance to BSA examiners that enhances their ability to perform risk-based BSA examinations of MSBs;

- Provide a resource to enhance the consistency of BSA examination procedures;

- Provide a summary of BSA compliance requirements and examination practices to the MSB industry; and

- Facilitate the efficient allocation of examination resources between federal and state BSA regulators.

Structure of Manual

In order to effectively apply resources and ensure compliance with BSA requirements, the manual is structured to allow examiners to tailor the BSA examination scope and procedures to the specific risk profile of the MSB under examination. The manual consists of the following sections:

- Introduction
- Examination Overview and Procedures for Assessing BSA Compliance
- Appendices

The overview sections provide narrative guidance and background information on each topic; each overview is followed by examination procedures. The "Examination Overview and Procedures" sections serve as a platform for the BSA examination. These sections address legal and regulatory requirements of the AML program centered on the effectiveness of the MSB's AML program and the MSB's compliance with the recordkeeping and reporting requirements of the BSA.

Not all of the examination procedures will be applicable to every MSB. The specific examination procedures that will need to be performed depend on the BSA/AML risk profile of the MSB, the quality and quantity of independent testing, the MSB's history of BSA compliance, and other relevant factors.

Within each section, the manual provides examination procedures for the examiner to follow, varying according to the risk profile identified during the pre-planning of the examination and the current examination findings. The examiner should perform the additional procedures outlined within each section to the extent necessary based on the risks identified. For example, if the examiner determines that a money transmitter may not have appropriate policies and procedures to ensure the reporting of all transactions requiring currency transaction reporting (e.g., no review of automated reports for currency transactions that exceed the reporting threshold), the examiner may decide that it is appropriate to sort transaction databases for a selected period of time to determine if transactions are being reported when required. The manual empowers the examiner to decide what examination procedures are necessary to evaluate whether the MSB's AML program is adequate to ensure compliance with requirements of the BSA.

This guide includes procedures for principal and agent MSB examinations. Some procedures pertain only to principal MSB examinations, where other procedures pertain only to agent MSB examinations or to both.

Money Services Business - Overview

Typical Structure of an MSB

MSBs can range from large sophisticated chains with interstate operations facilities that focus on providing a range of financial services such as check cashing and money transmission to small one-owner storefront operations that provide a few financial services, such as check cashing as an auxiliary service to its primary retail store operations. The business and management structure, as well as the overall risk profile, of an MSB can vary based on the size and complexity of the MSB. Some MSBs may engage in several different types of MSB-defined activities simultaneously. Some MSB-defined activities require more recordkeeping and reporting under the BSA than others do.

MSB chains may maintain several organizational levels to conduct business. Each level is authorized to approve certain size transactions. The number of authorization levels may vary depending on the dollar amounts of customer transactions and the number of branches. The principal employees can include the following (characteristics special to specific types of MSBs are discussed later):

- Director/Manager/Owner — Oversees the entire operation of the MSB. The manager may approve the largest currency transactions and may also be responsible for maintaining the internal control and records of the operations.

- Store Manager/Supervisor — Reviews daily teller work and reconciliations. The supervisor may approve medium-size transactions (for example, between $3,000 and $5,000), and often receives shipments of currency to and from the correspondent bank or other currency supplier. In addition, the supervisor may be charged with ensuring all transaction information required by federal and state recordkeeping requirements is obtained.

- Teller — Responsible for conducting all transactions and reconciling the total currency transactions to the teller's beginning and ending cash balances. The teller usually will have the lowest authorization for conducting currency transactions. The teller is the MSB's front line employee who should be aware enough of BSA regulations to perform duties such as securing information when appropriate from individuals conducting transactions that will trigger recordkeeping or currency transaction reporting requirements.

- BSA Compliance Officer — Responsible for implementing and monitoring the day-to-day BSA compliance and internal controls of the program. In a small business with only a few employees, the BSA compliance officer may execute all the tasks himself or herself. In a small business, duties may have to be discharged by a non-dedicated supervisor or employee. In a large, multi-state business, the BSA compliance officer will have supervisory responsibility over the AML program, and may have dedicated staff that performs specific duties related to BSA compliance. Some MSB chains may centralize the compliance and reporting function (so the central office will file all suspicious activity and currency transaction reports), while other MSBs with agent relationships prefer each agent to comply with its own recordkeeping and reporting obligations.

The special characteristics of the different types of MSBs are discussed in the sections that follow. The following sections provide an overview of common MSB business models, but are not meant to suggest that these are the only possible or even optimal structures. MSB operations will vary based on management's decisions on the controls appropriate for the MSB's unique business operations.

Branches and/or Agents

An MSB can provide more services to more customers through branches or agents. So an MSB may set up branches or enter into agent agreements with other commercial entities (like grocery stores, etc.) to establish portals that provide customers with convenient access to its locations and services.

What is the difference between a branch and an agent?

- Branches are "brick & mortar" locations where the MSB maintains an office, employs the staff directly, and is responsible for the operating costs of the branch, such as rent and utilities.[3]

- Conversely, in an agent relationship, the MSB enters into an agent service agreement with an independent entity, which in the vast majority of cases is another commercial entity that is seeking to add specific MSB services to its existing inventory of customer products and services. Many of the terms of the agreement or contract are generally stipulated by the state MSB regulations where the MSB is domiciled. Among other features, the agreement or contract typically sets forth the rights and obligations of both parties, as well as responsibilities for complying with all state and federal laws. Other important features include the fee structure and the fee remittance policy of the MSB. The advantage is that the cost of the agent agreement is generally an agreed upon service fee to be paid to the agent based upon the transactions the agent takes in. Using agents allows the MSB to expand its marketing network with less overhead requirements. As opposed to operating through a limited number of branch locations, constrained by costs, an MSB can enlist a network of agents to be able to reach a wider customer market.

---

3. If the MSB operates over the Internet, either in place of or in addition to offering services at a physical location, the location from which the MSB manages its Internet presence should be treated as a branch.

General Scope of the BSA Regulations

BSA regulations apply to certain industries (such as depository institutions, or broker-dealers in securities), certain activities (such as money transmission, or check cashing), or certain products offered by an industry (such as covered insurance products).

The BSA responsibilities of MSBs are activity-based: irrespective of the industry a person belongs to, or what the person labels as its main business activity, if the person performs certain specific activities in excess of a certain monetary threshold, then the person is an MSB for BSA purposes.

The BSA responsibilities associated with different MSB activities can be different. Therefore, a person that simultaneously engages in different MSB activities may be subject to different sets of recordkeeping and reporting requirements with respect to the different MSB activities. Such a person's BSA obligations will also depend on whether the person performs a particular MSB activity as an agent or as a principal.

Overview of Check Cashers

A check casher is defined as a person engaged in the business of cashing checks (other than a person who does not cash checks, money orders/traveler's checks or stored value in an amount greater than $1,000 in currency or other monetary instruments for any one person on any given day in one or more transactions). Such a person is an MSB, subject to applicable regulations.[4]

In many cases, the check casher acts as an agent of a money transmitter (or several money transmitters for different services, e.g., remittances, bill paying, and sale of money orders) to complement check cashing services.

Basic Model of a Check Casher

Check cashing services may be offered by a retail business, e.g., a grocery store, as an accommodation to its customers. However, the check casher may also be a stand-alone "brick and mortar" operation. Some check cashers focus solely on consumer check cashing and some focus on commercial check cashing. Check cashing operations may be located on the ground level in retail areas or industrial work areas, or close to residential areas, where there are limited or no banking facilities available. A check casher may be trying to serve the niche of the underserved or un-banked, in which case it will typically locate in a high foot traffic area to draw in customers.

---

4.   31 CFR 103.11(uu)(2).

Check cashers may provide a variety of financial services in order to allow one-stop shopping for financial services. For example, a customer that does not have a bank account works the second shift in an industrial area. In close proximity to work is a check cashing location. During his lunch hour, he goes over to the check casher to cash his payroll check of $1,200. While he is there he completes the following other financial transactions: a) buys a $500 money order to pay his rent, b) pays his electric bill of $200, c) transmits $200 to relatives in a foreign country, and d) receives the remaining $300 in cash. Thus, he is able to cash his check, and because the check casher is an agent for various money transmitters, he is able to buy a money order, pay a bill, and transmit money to relatives.

Overview of Currency Dealers or Exchangers

A currency dealer or exchanger (other than a person who does not exchange currency in an amount greater than $1,000 in currency or monetary or other instruments for any person on any day in one or more transactions) is defined as an MSB subject to all of the regulations applicable to MSBs.[5]

Currency dealers or exchangers provide many of the same services as banks and other regulated financial institutions. In addition to currency exchange, these services may include other MSB activities such as funds transmission (foreign and domestic), check cashing, the sale of money orders, or quasi-banking services such as maintaining temporary custody of funds on deposit.

Currency dealers or exchangers typically operate along international borders, in port of entry cities (where international flights land), or near communities of resident aliens. Some travel agencies will also operate as currency dealers or exchangers. A currency dealer or exchanger near the Southwest border or in a Hispanic area may be known as a "Casa de Cambio." For some currency dealers, small, personal, routine exchanges may be referred to as "retail" or "over the counter" transactions. Large transactions may be referred to as "vault" transactions.

Overview of Issuance, Sale, and Redemption of Money Orders/Traveler's Checks

An issuer of money orders or traveler's checks (money orders/traveler's checks), other than a person who does not issue such money orders/traveler's checks in an amount greater than $1,000 in currency or monetary or other instruments to any person on any day in one or more transactions, is defined as an MSB subject to all regulations applicable to MSBs.[6]

---

5.   31 CFR 103.11(uu)(1).

6.   31 CFR 103.11(uu)(3).

A seller or redeemer of money orders/traveler's checks (other than a person who does not sell or redeem such money orders/traveler's checks in an amount greater than $1,000 in currency or monetary or other instruments to any person on any day in one or more transactions) is also defined as an MSB subject to all regulations applicable to MSBs.[7]

Issuer or Redeemer

An issuer of a money order or traveler's check ("money order/traveler's check") is the business ultimately responsible for the payment of the money order or traveler's check.

A redeemer or seller is a business that exchanges money orders/traveler's checks (which it may or may not have issued) for currency or other instruments. The MSB definition in 31 CFR 103.11(u)(4) extends to "redeemers" of money orders and traveler's checks only insofar as the instruments involved are redeemed for monetary value – that is, for currency or monetary or other negotiable or other instruments. Taking a money order/traveler's check as payment for goods or general services is not redemption under BSA regulations.

Money orders/traveler's checks are generally issued by national companies. In addition, there are small regional or local money order/traveler's check issuers.

Some businesses, such as check cashers, may issue their own money orders. One example of a customer who typically buys money orders would be a person who does not have a bank account and who may use the instrument to pay bills. However, in some regions of the country it is not unusual for some businesses with bank accounts to buy money orders and use them to purchase wholesale merchandise.

Money orders and traveler's checks are negotiable monetary instruments sold through sales agents of money order/traveler's check issuers. Such agents may also provide other services such as check cashing or funds transmission that are ancillary to a primary business.

Issuers of money orders/traveler's checks may maintain proprietary branches that sell and redeem the issuer's money orders/traveler's checks. Issuers may also negotiate contracts with agents to sell the issuer's money orders/traveler's checks.

Sale of Money Orders/Traveler's Checks for National Companies

MSBs that sell money orders/traveler's checks for national companies (issuers) are agents. The agent's relationship to the issuer of the money orders/traveler's checks is governed by an agreement.

---

7. 31 CFR 103.11(uu)(4).

The agent is allowed to advertise money orders/traveler's checks that it sells and is authorized to fill in the dollar amount on behalf of the issuer.

- Money orders/traveler's checks are drawn on the issuer's bank account. The transaction is not complete until the issuer receives the face amount of the transaction from the agent and the money order/traveler's check clears the bank.

- The dollar value of a money order/traveler's check is generally limited by issuer policy; however, some agents may impose a more restrictive policy for individual and aggregate money order/traveler's check sales.

- The agent must maintain sales records of money orders/traveler's checks sold. Sales records typically include a unique transaction number and the money order/traveler's check serial number.

- The agent sends summary sales reports to its bank and to the issuer on a daily basis. The agent's bank then sends a clearing report to the issuer. The issuer downloads the bank sales and cleared reports, which are reconciled to the issuer's system generated reports. Exceptions, if any, are researched by the issuer and resolved with the agent.

- Money received from the sale of money orders/traveler's checks is usually deposited by the agent into a separate bank account, and must be deposited in accordance with issuer policy and applicable state regulations. The issuer's bank then sweeps the funds from the agent's bank account or, if the deposit account is owned by the issuer, the issuer-designated operating account.

National money order/traveler's check companies either collect their fee up front when the money orders/traveler's checks are given to the agents or upon periodic (e.g., weekly) settlement with the agent for money orders/traveler's checks sold. Commission statements are periodically (e.g., monthly) prepared by the issuer and provided to agents.

Identification of persons purchasing money orders/traveler's checks in amounts under $3,000 (there are recordkeeping requirements for all sales of money orders/traveler's checks between $3,000 and $10,000) are often left to the individual agents, but may be governed by the policies and procedures of the issuer (as principal MSB).

The issuer will retain front and back copies of all cleared and cancelled money orders/ traveler's checks, or delegates its clearing bank to do so.

Overview of a Money Transmitter

A money transmitter is defined as any person, whether or not licensed or required to be licensed, that engages as a business in accepting currency or funds denominated in currency and transmits the currency or funds, or the value of the currency or funds, by any means through a financial agency or institution, a Federal Reserve Bank or other facility of one or more Federal Reserve Banks, the Board of Governors of the Federal Reserve System, or both, or an electronic funds transfer network, or any person that is engaged as a business in the transfer of funds.[8]

Basic Business Model of a Money Transmitter

The basic money transmitter business model involves three parties:

| SENDER | → | MONEY TRANSMITTER | → | RECIPIENT |

The sender provides the funds to the money transmitter with instructions to deliver the funds to a recipient that the sender has identified to the money transmitter. The money transmitter conducts the transaction by taking the funds from the sender and delivering the funds to the recipient. This transfer of funds may be intrastate, interstate, or international. The money transmitter may send the funds through a formal funds transfer system (such as by electronic transfer) or through an informal funds transfer system (such as a hawala).

Large money transmitters may have a home office, transaction clearing center(s), service center(s), regional offices, and branches. They may also contract with agents. Agents may include established businesses such as grocery stores, truck stops, check cashers, pharmacists, travel agents, and supermarket chains. The money transmission home office pays its agents using a fee schedule that provides predetermined charges (fees) for money transmission. Agents receive a commission on the fees charged for transferring money. Some may receive a portion of any foreign exchange profit that may be received by the money transmitter.

When a transaction to send or to receive money is initiated by a sender, the money transmitter's employee or agent will contact the money transmitter's service center. This is generally done by dialing a toll-free number or by using an on-line computer system installed in the branch or agent location. The information from the sender transaction form is entered into the service center computer system. The origination transaction documents to send or to receive money are kept by the money transmitter anywhere from six months to five years or longer. The retention period is usually determined by the money transmission home office policies, as well as federal and state record retention requirements.

---

8.   31 CFR 103.11(uu)(5)(A) & (B).

Each money transmission company has its own forms to document sending and receiving money. Generally, the basic information recorded on these forms includes, but is not limited to:

- The date of the transaction;
- The amount of the transaction;
- The name of the person sending money (sender);
- The name of the person receiving the money (recipient); and
- The reference (transaction) number assigned by the service center.

BSA regulations require additional information to be obtained for transactions involving $3,000 or more.

Money transmitters may engage in money transmission for consumers and for commercial customers. A commercial money transmitter may engage in wholesale transactions with no agent network.

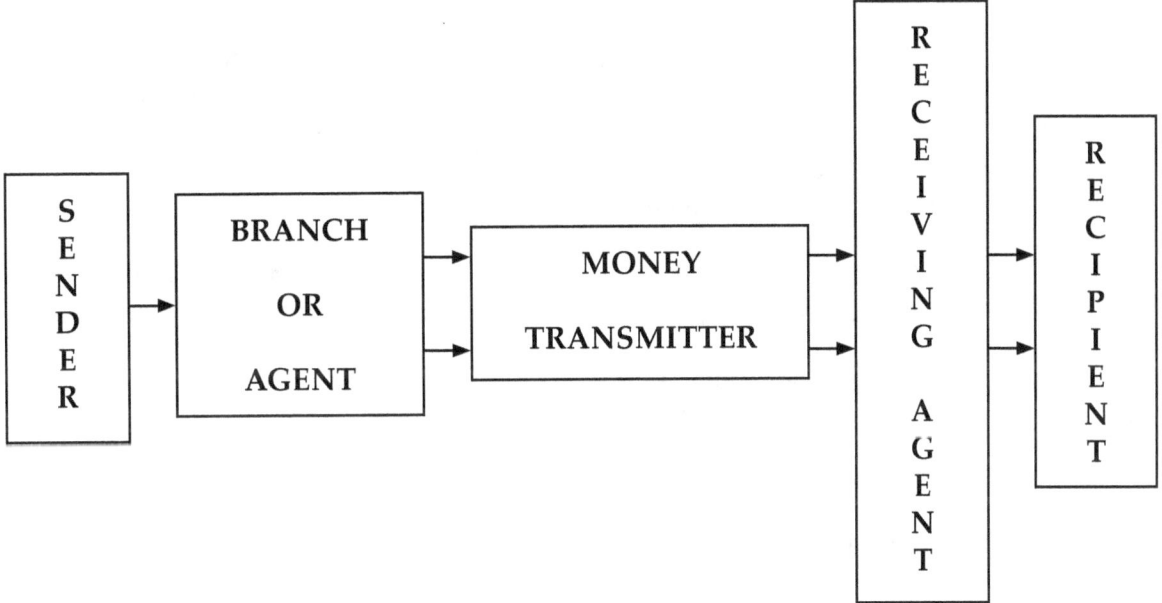

The diagram above adds two additional parties to the transaction: branches or agents, and receiving agents. Through branches and agents, money transmitters can expand customer access points. Attracting existing businesses, such as convenience stores, to act as agents allows the money transmitter to provide customer access and convenience while at the same time leveraging valuable and limited financial resources.

The money transmitter must have a means to deliver the funds to the recipient. Therefore, to be able to complete the transmission activity, the money transmitter will normally enter into agreements with receiving agents. Receiving agents are other financial service providers (including banks) that are in closer proximity to the recipient. Again, the relationship between the money transmitter and the receiving agent is contractual and the cost of the arrangement to the money transmitter is fee-based.

Transaction Flow of a Money Transmitter

A money transmitter has established a network of agent relationships. A sender enters one of the agent locations and wishes to send $500 to a recipient in another location. The sender provides the agent the funds and instructions for delivery to the recipient. The agent takes the funds and instructions and usually enters the transaction into a computer terminal owned by the money transmitter. The terminal is linked to the money transmitter's processing system. Upon receiving the instructions, the money transmitter will contact its appropriate receiving agent for payout to the recipient. The sender and/or the receiving agent will inform the recipient that the transmitted funds are available for pick-up. The availability of funds to the recipient may range from minutes to several days depending upon the location and availability of the receiving agent and the money transmitter's delivery policy as disclosed to the sender.

An elaborate computer system is not necessary to conduct money transmission transactions. Telephone lines and fax machines are still widely used as cost effective substitutes for transmitting money. However, the larger and more complex the money transmitter, the more likely the use of technology to improve transaction and compliance controls as well as agent accounting.

A notable aspect of transaction flow is the timing difference that can occur between the receipt of sender funds by the money transmitter and the delivery (or availability) of those funds to the recipient. If the sender came into the agent location at 10:00 a.m. and the recipient was able to receive the funds by 2:00 p.m. the same day, then it is probable that the agent had not deposited the sender's funds to the money transmitter's bank account by the time funds were made available to the recipient by the money transmitter. The money transmitter had, in effect, paid the recipient before receiving bank credit for the sender's funds. This may be referred to as "reverse float" or "negative float."

For example, at 10:00 a.m. ABC Money Transmitter's agent, XYZ Grocery Store receives funds from a customer for transmission to Mexico City. ABC Money Transmitter's receiving agent in Mexico City is able to pay the funds to the recipient by 2:00 p.m.; however, XYZ Grocery Store has not yet sent to funds to ABC Money Transmitter. ABC Money Transmitter has fronted the funds for the transmission and will be reimbursed when the initial funds for the transaction received by XYZ Grocery Store are sent on to ABC Money Transmitter. For the transaction to be completed, XYZ Grocery Store, the sending agent, must deposit the funds received from the sender into its bank account. This is usually a designated trust account of ABC Money Transmitter, but there are also cases where the agent service agreement may allow for deposit into another account of the agent, such as a general business account. ABC Money Transmitter via its computer system knows how many transactions (and their aggregate amount) that the agent has executed, and the money transmitter then sweeps the funds it is owed into its accounts (typically by automated clearing house) on a daily basis or as required. *This is a critical point. In this type of structure, a money transmitter and its agent must both have access to the banking system.*

Overview of Principal and Agent MSB Relationships

A principal MSB includes the "issuer" of money orders/traveler's checks or the "provider" of the transmission service. A principal MSB may provide its services through numerous agent relationships. In an agent relationship, the principal MSB may not have control over other financial services provided by its agents outside the agency agreement.

Agent MSBs may have one location (such as a corner convenience store with only one location) or may have a network of locations that provide agent services (such as a grocery store or pharmacy chain, where the chain offers money orders and/or funds transmittals as an agent of a principal MSB). An agent MSB may act solely as an agent of an MSB or may offer additional services, such as check cashing, as a principal MSB. An agent may also contract with different principal MSBs to offer services. For example, an agent may sell money orders as an agent of a money order issuer and may also offer money transmission services as an agent of a money transmitter. An agent could also act as an agent for more than one money transmitter.

Each MSB, whether an agent or a principal MSB, is responsible for compliance with BSA requirements, including the establishment of an anti-money laundering program, currency transaction reporting, and suspicious activity reporting; however, an agent MSB and a principal MSB may allocate compliance responsibility between each. Note: Both the principal and the agent remain independently responsible for implementation of the requirements of the BSA, and nothing in 31 CFR 103.125 relieves any MSB from its obligations to establish and maintain an effective AML program.

EXAMINATION OVERVIEW AND PROCEDURES FOR ASSESSING BSA COMPLIANCE

Objective: *The MSB Examination Manual is intended to offer guidance to BSA Examiners regarding Title 31 – Bank Secrecy Act examinations. While one of the goals of this manual is to develop and enhance uniform BSA examination procedures, it is not intended to replace an examiner's independent judgment.*

Under Title 31, MSBs are a sub-group of non-bank financial institutions that are not comprehensively regulated by a federal banking regulator, the Securities and Exchange Commission, or the Commodity Futures Trading Commission. Given the variety of businesses covered under the Bank Secrecy Act as MSBs and the wide range of accounting and recordkeeping systems utilized by these institutions, examination steps need to be applicable to a wide variety of situations.

The BSA examination consists of five phases:

1. Pre-planning
2. On-site visit to the business and interview of appropriate personnel
3. Examination of the AML program
4. Examination of the books and records of the business
5. Developing conclusions and finalizing the exam

The adequacy of the MSB's BSA compliance is the BSA examiner's primary focus. The BSA examiner must review the AML program, internal processes, and records to determine the adequacy of the AML program. In order to assess the effectiveness of the MSB's AML program and its compliance with BSA regulatory requirements, the BSA examiner can utilize various risk-based examination procedures and techniques. The techniques outlined below constitute a general guide to examination activity, which should be modified when appropriate.

Risk-Based Approach to BSA Examinations

To ensure that MSBs have in place the processes necessary to identify, measure, monitor, and control risk exposures, examinations have increasingly emphasized evaluating the appropriateness of these processes. While the examiner will always perform some transactional testing under a risk-based examination approach, the amount of transaction testing will be reduced when the examiner determines that internal risk-management processes are adequate or risks are minimal. However, when risk-management processes or internal controls are considered inappropriate, such as when there is an inadequate segregation of duties or when on-site testing determines that necessary processes are inadequate or absent, additional transaction testing should be performed. In addition, if an examiner believes that an MSB's management is being less than candid, has provided false or misleading information, or has omitted material information, then substantial on-site transaction testing should be performed.

An effective risk-based BSA examination program will cover an MSB's major activities. The frequency and depth of each area's examination procedures will vary according to the risk assessment of that area. Examiners should determine the appropriate depth and scope of the examination procedures based on their assessment of the risks of the MSB. The examination phases build on each other, as well as on the facts determined at each stage of the examination. For example, if the examiner has not been able to gather enough information during the pre-plan stage to make a complete risk assessment of the MSB, then the examiner should conduct extensive interviews to perform a complete risk assessment onsite. If the MSB does not have an AML program or the program is not based on the risks that actually apply to the particular MSB, then an examiner should conduct extensive interviews and perform more extensive transaction tests to determine whether and to what extent the MSB is in violation of BSA requirements.

Principal MSB Examinations Versus Agent MSB Examinations

Examinations of principal MSBs have some unique issues that are not present in the examinations of MSBs acting as agents of a principal MSB. These include:

- Selection, monitoring, and termination of agents;
- Ensuring the principal MSB's services are not being used to launder money or circumvent the BSA requirements;
- Conducting due diligence reviews of foreign agents or foreign counterparties;
- For an issuer of money orders/traveler's checks, the identification of potential suspicious activity based on a review of clearance records; and
- The identification of transactions conducted by multiple agents that may require reporting under the BSA, such as cash transactions with multiple agents of a money transmitter where the aggregated transactions through the principal MSB total more than $10,000 for one customer in a single day, but the transactions through *any one agent* are less than $10,000 for one customer in one day.

An MSB that acts solely as an agent for another MSB (principal MSB) may enter into an agreement with the principal MSB that allocates between them responsibility for development of policies, procedures, and internal controls. Alternatively, agent MSBs may follow the principal MSB's internal controls for handling, recording, and reporting transactions. Whose standards apply should be considered in an examination of the agent MSB. For example, an agent of a money transmitter may follow the principal's procedures for reporting applicable currency transactions. This could include procedures that require the principal MSB to file applicable CTRs for currency received and disbursed by the agent.

Differences in examinations of principal MSBs and agent MSBs will be outlined as applicable in the various sections of this manual.

Pre-Planning the BSA Examination — Overview

Objective: *Identify the MSB's BSA/AML risks, develop the examination scope, and document the plan. This process includes determining examination needs for staffing and technical expertise, and selecting examination procedures to be completed.*

The BSA examination is intended to assess the MSB's compliance with the regulatory requirements pertaining to the BSA, in particular the effectiveness of the MSB's AML program. It is important to keep in mind that this is distinct from the goal of a safety and soundness examination – to assess the financial health of the MSB – particularly because many states conduct both types of examinations at the same time.

In planning the BSA examination, the examiner should attempt to gather as much information as possible before meeting with the MSB in order to gain an understanding of the business, make a preliminary risk assessment, identify potential money laundering risks, and identify appropriate examination procedures based upon the preliminary risk assessment of the business. This will maximize the effectiveness of the examination.

Whenever possible, the pre-planning process should be completed before entering the MSB. During this process, it may be helpful to discuss BSA matters with the MSB's management, including the BSA compliance officer. The scoping and planning process begins with an analysis of:

- Historical information;
- Prior examination reports, correspondence, and work papers;
- BSA-reporting databases (Web Currency and Banking Retrieval System (Web CBRS)), in order to determine if the MSB has registered with FinCEN, as well as whether the MSB has filed any BSA reports or been the subject of reports filed by other entities;
- The MSB's BSA/AML risk assessment and "registrant profile";
- Independent reviews or audits; and
- Business structure, including (if applicable) whether the MSB maintains branches and/or agent relationships.

Information Available from FinCEN Database (Web CBRS)

Examination planning should include an analysis of the Suspicious Activity Reports for Money Services Business (SAR-MSBs), Currency Transaction Reports (CTRs), Reports of International Transportation of Currency or Monetary Instruments (CMIRs), Reports of Foreign Bank and Financial Accounts (FBARs), and Registration of MSB (RMSB) relating to the MSB. With authorized access, SAR-MSBs, CTRs, FBARs, CMIRs and RMSB may be downloaded or obtained directly on-line from the FinCEN database maintained by the IRS Enterprise Computing Center—Detroit (ECC-D)[9] , which is commonly known as the Web Currency and Banking Retrieval System (Web CBRS). Information can be downloaded into an electronic spreadsheet, which contains all of the data included on the original document filed by the MSB as well as the IRS Document Control Number (DCN), and the date the document was entered into Web CBRS. Downloaded information is important to the examination, as it will help examiners determine the filing history of the MSB by reviewing the:

- Volume of transactions between the MSB and its banks or other financial institutions and the volume of CTRs filed on the MSB;
- Volume of CTRs in relation to the number of agents/branches;
- Volume of CTRs filed by the MSB;
- Volume of SAR-MSBs in relation to the number of agents/branches;
- Volume of SAR-MSBs filed by the MSB;
- Volume of SARs filed on the MSB;
- Consistency of filings by the MSB or lack of filings; and
- Initial MSB registration, re-registration (if applicable), and the frequency of filing MSB renewal registration.

Based upon the results of the review, the examiner should be able to:

- Identify customers who perform transactions involving high dollar volumes of currency;
- Assist in selecting customers for transaction testing;
- Identify the number and characteristics of SAR-MSBs filed;
- Determine if any incomplete or inaccurate documents were filed; and
- Determine whether there is a history of filing errors that might appear to be systemic.

---

9. The IRS ECC-D was formerly known as the Detroit Computing Center.

Risk Assessment

Each MSB's AML program must be commensurate with the risks posed by the location and size of the particular MSB, and by the nature and volume of the financial services it offers. Each MSB should identify and assess the money laundering risks that may be associated with its unique combination of products, services, customers, geographic locations, etc. Regardless of where risks arise, MSBs must take reasonable steps to manage them. Each MSB should focus resources on the areas of its business that management believes pose the greatest risks. Although MSBs are not required by regulation to create a written risk assessment, management is encouraged to document its risk assessment in writing in order to provide a clear basis for the MSB's policies and procedures. If the MSB does not have a written risk assessment, the examiner will generally need to conduct more in depth interviews in order to determine the MSB's risk profile.[10]

The AML program, however, must be written and must address the following four "pillars" of a sound AML program:

- Internal controls based upon the MSB's risk assessment, which are designed to detect and deter money laundering and terrorist financing;

- Designate a BSA compliance officer and detail the role he/she will play in the day-to-day supervision of the MSB;

- Provide for and document policies and procedures to perform independent testing of the MSB to measure compliance with the BSA; and

- Provide for and document BSA/AML training for appropriate personnel.

The risk-based nature of the AML program requirement is designed to give an MSB flexibility to tailor its AML program to specific circumstances. For example, the AML program for an MSB that provides a wide range of financial services (e.g., check cashing, currency exchange, money order sales, and money transmission services) from multiple branches would be structured differently from an AML program for an MSB that offers one or two services through an agent network. In addition, an MSB that offers multiple financial services may need to offer more comprehensive training for employees to recognize aspects of suspicious activity that may be associated with different transaction types and that may differ based on the geographic location of branches and/or agents. An MSB with multiple locations and/or agents that regularly offers multiple financial services may require more extensive oversight by its compliance officer than would an MSB that offers one or two financial services incidental to its core business. The former would also require a more frequent independent review.

---

10. The BSA provisions of Title 31 do not require the risk assessment to be documented in writing.

The risk assessment process enables MSB management to better identify and mitigate gaps in BSA/AML controls. There are many effective methods and formats used in completing a BSA/AML risk assessment. MSB management should decide the appropriate method or format, based on the MSB's risk profile. MSB management should ensure that all appropriate parties can easily understand the format of the risk assessment.

The development of the BSA/AML risk assessment generally involves identifying the specific risk categories (i.e., products, customers, geographic locations, etc.) that are unique to the MSB, and then conducting a more detailed analysis of these categories as they apply to the MSB in order to assess the risk associated with each risk category. A detailed analysis will provide MSB management with a better understanding of the MSB's risk profile in order to develop appropriate policies, procedures, and processes to mitigate risks.

Identifying Specific Risk Categories

An MSB's risk categories will vary depending on the MSB. The risk categories below are not exhaustive; however, they provide examples of risk categories the MSB should consider when performing its risk assessment.

Product Risk

Offering certain products and services such as those that offer customers more anonymity or involve the handling of high dollar volumes of currency or currency equivalents, may pose greater risk of money laundering or terrorist financing to an MSB. For example, sales of traveler's checks, sales of money orders, and transmittals of funds may be particularly vulnerable to structuring (the breaking up of a transaction into multiple transactions to fall beneath the thresholds for recordkeeping and reporting). An effective AML program for an MSB significantly engaged in such activities would include the training of employees to recognize indications of structuring.

Customer Risk

Although any customer could conceivably be engaged in money laundering or terrorist financing, certain customers may pose heightened risk because of the nature of their business, occupation, or anticipated transaction activity. In assessing customer risk, MSBs should consider variables such as the type of money services sought and the geographic locations involved in transactions. Potential questions that MSBs should consider when assessing their customer risk may include:

- Who are the customers?
- What do they use the service or product for?
- How do they pay for the service or product?
- What is an average transaction?

- How frequently does the customer purchase the service or product?
- When is the customer most likely to need the service or product?
- What is the typical daily or monthly volume?

Geographic Risk

Identifying geographic locations that may pose a higher risk of money laundering or terrorist financing is essential to an MSB's risk assessment. MSBs should understand and evaluate the specific risks associated with doing business in, processing transactions for customers from, or facilitating transactions involving certain geographic locations.

High-risk geographic locations can be either international or domestic. International high-risk geographic locations generally include:

- Countries, jurisdictions and governments subject to OFAC sanctions, including state sponsors of terrorism;[11]
- Countries identified as supporting international terrorism under section 6(j) of the Export Administration Act of 1979, as determined by the Secretary of State;[12]
- Jurisdictions determined to be "of primary money laundering concern" by the Secretary of the Treasury, and jurisdictions subject to special measures imposed by the Secretary of the Treasury, through FinCEN, pursuant to section 311 of the USA PATRIOT Act; [13]
- Countries and territories identified as non-cooperative by the Financial Action Task Force (FATF);[14] and
- Major money laundering countries and jurisdictions identified in the U.S. Department of State's annual International Narcotics Control Strategy Report (INCSR), in particular, countries that are identified as jurisdictions of primary concern.[15]

---

11. A list of such countries, jurisdictions, and governments is available on OFAC's web site: www.treas.gov/ofac.

12. A list of the countries supporting international terrorism appears in the U.S. Department of State's annual *Country Reports on Terrorism*. This report is available on the U.S. Department of State's web site for its Counterterrorism Office: www.state.gov/s/ct/.

13. Notices of proposed rulemaking and final rules accompanying the determination of "primary money laundering concern" and imposition of a special measure (or measures) pursuant to section 311 of the USA PATRIOT Act are available on the FinCEN web site: www.fincen.gov/reg_section311.html.

14. A current list of countries designated by FATF as non-cooperative countries and territories (NCCT) is available on the FATF web site: www.fatf-gafi.org.

15. The INCSR, including the lists of high-risk money laundering countries and jurisdictions, may be accessed on the U.S. Department of State's Bureau of International Narcotics and Law Enforcement Affairs web page http://www.state.gov/p/inl/rls/nrcrpt/.

Domestic high-risk geographic locations may include, but are not limited to, a U.S. Government–designated high-risk geographic location. Domestic high-risk geographic locations include both High Intensity Drug Trafficking Areas (HIDTAs)[16] and High Intensity Financial Crime Areas (HIFCAs).[17]

Operational Risk

Operational risk is the risk that an MSB will fail to detect or prevent money laundering or terrorist financing as a result of inadequate internal processes or systems, or as a result of human failure. Evaluation of operational risk includes:

- The MSB's systems used to process transactions that utilize transactional dollar limitations;
- The frequency of agent or employee turnover;
- The recordkeeping system utilized by the MSB;
- The activities of the MSB. (MSBs whose activities include both financial and non-financial products and services such as retail stores who cash checks);
- The MSB's business structure and business plan;
- The involvement of senior management in BSA matters; and
- The MSB's agent relationships.

Management should consider the staffing resources and the level of training necessary to promote adherence with policies, procedures, and processes. For those MSBs that have taken on a higher-risk BSA/AML profile, management should address this in the risk assessment and provide a more robust program that specifically monitors and controls the higher risks that management and the board have accepted.

Analysis of Specific Risk Categories

The level and sophistication of analysis may vary from one MSB to another because of the varying risks of products, services, customers, etc. The detailed analysis is important because within any type of product, service, category of customer, etc., there are varying levels of risk. A detailed analysis will help the MSB implement appropriate policies, procedures, and processes to mitigate risks.

---

16. The Anti-Drug Abuse Act of 1988 and The Office of National Drug Control Policy (ONDCP) Reauthorization Act of 1998 authorized the Director of ONDCP to designate areas within the United States that exhibit serious drug trafficking problems and harmfully impact other areas of the country as HIDTAs. The HIDTA Program provides additional federal resources to those areas to help eliminate or reduce drug trafficking and its harmful consequences. A listing of these areas can be found at http://www.whitehousedrugpolicy.gov.

17. HIFCAs were first announced in the 1999 National Money Laundering Strategy and were conceived in the Money Laundering and Financial Crimes Strategy Act of 1998 as a means of concentrating law enforcement efforts at the federal, state, and local levels in high intensity money laundering zones. A listing of these areas can be found at http://www.fincen.gov/hifcaregions.html.

A money transmitter may perform the following analysis:

The MSB transmits 1,000 international funds transmittals per day. The analysis may show that 85 percent of the transactions are done face-to-face through a branch location. On the other hand, the analysis may show that 85 percent of these transmittals are not done face-to-face, but are done through the internet. While the number of transactions is the same for these two examples, the overall risks are different. The MSB can implement policies, procedures, and internal controls to mitigate these risks. For example, the MSB may limit the number and dollar amount of transactions that can be done online within a certain time period. The examiner's evaluation of the MSB's risk assessment along with implemented policies, procedures, and internal controls will help the examiner determine the scope of the examination. An MSB that has implemented appropriate policies, procedures, and internal controls to mitigate its risks may require less transactional testing during the examination.

Review of the MSB BSA/AML Risk Assessment

The scoping and planning process should be guided by the examiner's review of the MSB's BSA/AML risk assessment. Information gained from the examiner's review of the risk assessment will assist the examination pre-planning process, as well as the evaluation of the adequacy of the AML program. For the purposes of the examination, whenever the MSB has not completed a risk assessment, or the risk assessment is inadequate, the examiner will need to prepare a risk assessment in effect on behalf of the MSB (a process that will be discussed in more detail in the next section on examiner development of a BSA/AML risk assessment) in order to be able to complete the examination.

The examiner should review the MSB's risk assessment to determine whether management has considered and adequately assessed all products, services, customers, geographic locations, etc.

When reviewing the MSB's risk assessment, an examiner should not look at one factor independent from other factors in order to determine the MSB's risk level. For example, the MSB may receive a very high volume of money transmissions. The transmission volume alone does not necessarily indicate high risk, but the locations from which the funds are received could impact the risk associated with the activity and may need to be considered more. When reviewing the MSB's risk assessment, the examiner should determine whether management has developed an accurate risk assessment that identifies the significant risks to the MSB.

An important element of the AML program analysis should include whether the MSB considered how the risk of money laundering could impact its business and how it should have addressed this risk as part of its AML program. This includes identification and consideration of all risk categories the MSB faces. Internal and external audits and reviews, corporate or business board minutes, internal memoranda, etc., that specifically address BSA policies, procedures, or operations should also be examined for their impact on BSA compliance.

The appropriateness of the MSB's risk assessment and implemented AML program will help the examiner determine the scope of the examination, including the amount of transaction testing that will need to be performed.

Examiner Development of a BSA/AML Risk Assessment

In some situations, MSBs may not have performed or completed an adequate BSA/AML risk assessment.[18] Examiners must address the need to complete a risk assessment when the MSB has not done so, or when the MSB faces unique risks not addressed in its AML program. Examiners should ensure that they have a general understanding of the MSB's BSA/AML risks, and at a minimum should document these risks within the examination scoping process. The risk assessment developed by examiners generally will not be as comprehensive as the one developed by the MSB. However, examiners should obtain information on the MSB's products, services, customers, geographic locations, etc., to identify potentially higher-risk areas. This process can begin with an analysis of:

- BSA-reporting database information (Web Currency and Banking Retrieval System (Web CBRS));
- Prior examination or inspection reports and workpapers;
- Response to request letter items; and
- Discussions with MSB management.

Examiners should complete this analysis by reviewing the level and trend of information pertaining to the MSB's activities identified, for example:

- Transmittal of funds
- Check cashing
- Money order/traveler's check sales
- Agent relationships
- Branch locations
- Domestic and international geographic locations of the MSB's business area

The examiner should evaluate information related to the MSB's activities (e.g., types of check cashing activities, limits on check cashing, agent relationships, or receiving locations for money transmission) in relation to due diligence performed by the MSB (e.g., customer due diligence or agent due diligence).

---

18. The BSA provisions of Title 31 do not require the risk assessment to be documented in writing.

A risk assessment requires a careful consideration of the facts applicable to the MSB and utilizes the examiner's judgment and experience of the likelihood of the MSB being used to launder money or finance terrorism. Potential areas to review in order to develop a risk assessment include the following:

- The likelihood that the MSB's activities could result in money laundering or facilitating terrorist financing activities;

- Transaction cycles or financial activities that do not have internal controls in place to prevent, detect, or limit the risk that the MSB could be used to facilitate money laundering or terrorist financing activities; and

- The likelihood of an event such as the loss of electronic records occurring combined with the failure of internal controls to prevent or eliminate the risks of a BSA violation (the vulnerability of internal controls).

This information should be evaluated relative to such factors as the MSB's size, customer base, products, services, geographic locations, etc. Examiners should exercise caution if comparing information between MSBs and use their experience and insight when performing this analysis. Specifically, examiners should avoid comparing the number of SAR-MSBs filed by an MSB to those filed by another MSB in the same geographic location. Examiners can and should use their knowledge of the risks associated with products, services, customers, geographic locations, etc., to help them determine the MSB's BSA/AML risk profile. Refer to Appendix C – Risk Matrix when completing this evaluation.

After identifying potential high-risk operations, examiners should form a preliminary BSA/AML risk profile of the MSB. The preliminary risk profile will provide the examiner with the basis for the initial BSA examination scope and the ability to determine the adequacy of the MSB's AML program. MSBs may have high-risk activities, but an effective AML program tailored to those specific risks should appropriately mitigate the risks.

The examiner may not have enough information to perform a preliminary risk assessment in the pre-planning phase of the exam. Additional facts may be gathered from the interview, on-site observation of the business, review of the MSB's AML program, and the results of transaction testing.

Examination workpapers should include any risk assessment provided by the MSB, the deficiencies noted in the MSB's risk assessment, and any examiner-prepared risk assessment.

Developing a Risk-Based Examination Plan

The examiner should develop an initial examination scoping and planning document commensurate with the preliminary BSA/AML risk profile. The scoping and planning process should ensure that the examiner is aware of the MSB's AML program, compliance history, and risk profile (i.e., products, services, customers, geographic locations, etc.). While the examination plan may change at any time as a result of on-site findings, the initial risk assessment will enable the examiner to establish a reasonable scope for the BSA examination. For the examination process to be successful, examiners should maintain open communication with the MSB's management and discuss relevant concerns as they arise. As appropriate, the examiner should contact MSB management, including the BSA compliance officer, to discuss the following:

- AML program
- BSA management structure
- BSA/AML risk assessment
- BSA/AML independent review

Once the risks applicable to the MSB have been identified, the examiner can begin to plan the scope and depth of the examination. Specifically, the examiner should first address the overall risks of the MSB, and then decide upon examination procedures to address those risks as they apply to the products and services that the MSB provides to the public.

Once an examiner has identified the MSB's risks, then the examiner should analyze the procedures contained within the AML program and any other desk guides that may be part of the MSB's policies to ensure that these risks are mitigated. The BSA examiner's examination plan, including transactional testing and analysis, should be based on the risks identified. As necessary, additional transaction testing may be completed. For example, if an MSB does not have an AML program, then an examiner may perform the additional examination steps outlined in this manual to identify the extent of BSA violations that may have occurred.

A risk-based BSA examination should consider factors that include:

- The relationship between the MSB's risk assessment and the AML program policies and procedures through which the MSB addresses those risks. For example, does the MSB have policies and procedures regarding the SAR-MSB reporting requirements that reasonably relate to the MSB's products, services, and customer activities?

- The results of the examiner's review of the MSB's risk assessment or the results of the examiner's risk assessment. High risks require more examination resources. How does the examiner plan to address the BSA/AML risks of the MSB?

- Any differences between the examiner's risk assessment and the MSB's risk assessment.

- Whether the MSB's written AML program meets the requirements of the Bank Secrecy Act (the four pillars).

- Potential examination procedures to test the BSA/AML policies and procedures of the MSB. For example, what are the MSB's procedures for filing CTRs and SAR-MSBs? What are the MSB's procedures to ensure appropriate records are obtained for sales of money orders/traveler's checks? Were forms timely filed and records obtained according to the MSB's procedures?

Considering these factors allows the examiner to develop a system of examination procedures to verify if the internal controls of the MSB have been implemented and are operating as designed.

The examination may focus on one or more financial services based upon the MSB's risk assessment, recent independent review, and prior examination findings. The examiner should document the factors used in choosing to perform fewer examination procedures for a particular financial service. For example, in connection with a decision not to review an MSB's check cashing services, the examiner might note that check cashing is a minimal service for the MSB where a low maximum check cashing limit has been established. Minimal testing can be done in situations like these to document the MSB's adherence to its self-imposed limitations.

BSA Examination Program Elements

A risk-based BSA examination program increases examination efficiency and effectiveness. Utilizing a risk-based approach, examiners can focus on the aspects of the MSB that are the highest risk and gain an understanding of whether the MSB is knowledgeable about the BSA and its specific requirements. To ensure that MSBs have in place the processes necessary to identify, measure, monitor, and control risk exposures, examinations have increasingly emphasized evaluating the appropriateness of these processes, evolving away from a high degree of transaction testing. Under a risk-based examination approach, the amount of transaction testing should be reduced when internal risk-management processes are determined to be adequate or when risks are minimal. The sophistication and formality of risk-based exams will vary depending on the MSB's size and complexity. To determine the appropriate level of examination coverage for the MSB environment, the examiner should assess the MSB's risk. This risk assessment should provide the examiner with objective information to prioritize the allocation of examination resources. A risk-based BSA examination program should:

- Identify the MSB's AML program, internal control policies and procedures, BSA personnel, data, transactional and operating systems, technology, and physical locations;

- Identify the MSB's business activities and processes;

- Include profiles of significant business units (HQ, branches and/or agents), products and services, and their associated BSA risks and control features; and

- Generate a document that describes and evaluates the structure of risk and controls throughout the MSB.

Transaction Testing

Examiners perform transaction testing (using a sample of transactions) to evaluate the adequacy of the MSB's compliance with regulatory requirements, to determine the effectiveness of its policies, procedures, and processes, and to evaluate suspicious activity monitoring systems. Transaction testing is another important factor in forming conclusions about the integrity of the MSB's overall controls and risk management processes. Transaction testing should be risk-based.

The extent of transaction testing and activities conducted is based on various factors, including the examiner's judgment of risks, controls, and the adequacy of the independent testing. Once on-site, the scope of the transaction testing can be adjusted to address any issues or concerns identified during the pre-plan examination stage. Examiners should document their decision regarding the extent of transaction testing, the activities for which it is to be performed, and the rationale for any changes to the scope of transaction testing that occur during the examination.

Testing should be sufficient to assess the degree of risk exposure in a particular function or activity. When risk management processes or internal controls are considered inappropriate, such as when there is an inadequate segregation of duties or when on-site testing determines that necessary processes are inadequate or absent, additional transaction testing should be performed. In addition, if an examiner believes that an MSB's management is being less than candid, has provided false or misleading information, or has omitted material information, then substantial on-site transaction testing should be performed.

Examination Procedures
Pre-Planning the BSA Examination

The goal of a BSA examination is to make a determination of whether the MSB is in compliance with the Bank Secrecy Act. FinCEN and the regulatory community recognize that not all MSBs are subject to the same risk. Therefore, examination procedures will vary depending on the examiner's assessment of the MSB's risks.

To facilitate the examiner's understanding of the MSB's risk profile and to adequately establish the scope of the BSA examination, the examiner should consider the factors identified in this section, in addition to those required by applicable state statutes, in conjunction with the review of the MSB's BSA/AML risk assessment.

Pre-Plan Procedures

1. Conduct preliminary research on the MSB. Research should include ownership, corporate structure, number of branches, number of agents, and "doing business as" (d/b/a) or "also known as" (a/k/a) information. This helps the examiner identify the examination scope and the potential risk of non-compliance. Consider reviewing news articles concerning the MSB or its management and employees. Thoroughly review public records, internet sources, etc., to determine if there are any related entities with common ownership. Evaluate whether the MSB has any increased BSA/AML risks due to the relationship(s) and how management has addressed these risks.

2. Obtain and review as applicable, from other state agencies and/or the IRS, prior examination reports, related workpapers, and management's responses to previously identified BSA violations, deficiencies, weaknesses, and recommendations. Review prior examination workpapers to identify the specific BSA examination procedures completed, report titles, previously noted violations, the cause of the violations, and any written statements indicating corrective action the MSB has taken. As necessary, discuss any additional information or ongoing concerns that are not documented in the correspondence with the examiner(s) responsible for prior examinations.

3. If the MSB is under a supervisory action, review the requirements of the action. Review correspondence concerning management's corrective actions.

4. Send a request letter for documents to the MSB. Review the request letter documents provided by the MSB. Refer to Appendix D – Sample Request Letter and Documents for MSBs.

5. Obtain and evaluate any independent reviews, along with supporting documents. The scope and quality of the independent review(s) may provide examiners with a sense of particular risks in the MSB, how these risks are being managed and controlled, and the MSB's response to identified weaknesses. The independent review workpapers can assist examiners in understanding the review coverage and the quality and quantity of prior transaction testing. This knowledge will assist the examiner in determining the examination scope, identifying areas requiring greater (or lesser) scrutiny, and identifying when expanded examination procedures may be necessary. Assess the adequacy of the information in the reports relating to BSA compliance. Determine if the independent review formed appropriate conclusions and remedies of all matters relating to BSA compliance. (Refer to the Anti-Money Laundering Program - Overview and Anti-Money Laundering Program - Examination Procedures sections of this manual for additional information on reviewing an MSB's independent review.)

6. As appropriate, contact MSB management, including the BSA compliance officer, to engage in initial discussions of the following (refer to the appropriate overview and examination procedures sections in this manual for guidance on these topics):

   • AML program;

   • BSA management structure;

   • BSA/AML risk assessment;

   • Suspicious activity monitoring and reporting systems; and

   • Level and extent of automated BSA systems.

7. Review correspondence that the MSB or the primary regulator(s) have received from, or sent to, outside regulatory and law enforcement agencies relating to BSA compliance. Communications, particularly those received from FinCEN and the Internal Revenue Service (IRS) Enterprise Computing Center (ECC-D), may document matters relevant to the examination such as:

   • Filing errors for SAR-MSBs and CTRs

   • Administrative actions or civil money penalties issued or being considered by FinCEN or other supervisory agencies

   • Law enforcement prosecutions, subpoenas or seizures

8. Determine if any related entities are currently under BSA examination. Consider obtaining information relevant to that examination and evaluate any identified weaknesses when considering the scope of the examination. Information may be obtained through memoranda of understanding with other state or federal regulatory agencies.

9. Subject to authorized access to Web CBRS, review the SAR-MSBs, CTRs, CMIRs, FBARs, and RSMB relating to the MSB. The number of SAR-MSBs, CTRs, CMIRs, and FBARs filed should be obtained for a defined time period, as determined by the

examiner. The information should be used to assist in assessing the filing history of the MSB and the risk profile of the MSB. This information can help determine whether the MSB has adequate internal controls, policies, and procedures related to the BSA.

- Determine the filing history of the MSB, by reviewing the:
    - Volume of transactions between the MSB and its bank or other financial institutions and the volume of CTRs filed on the MSB;
    - Volume of CTRs in relation to the number of agents/branches;
    - Volume of CTRs filed by the MSB in relation to the MSB's size, assets and geographic location;
    - Volume of SAR-MSBs in relation to the number of agents/branches;
    - Volume of SAR-MSBs filed by the MSB in relation to the MSB's size, assets and geographic location;
    - Volume of SARs filed on the MSB;
    - Consistency of filings by the MSB or lack of filings; and
    - Frequency of filing registrations.

- Identify high-volume and frequent currency customers. An increased number of high-volume currency customers may increase the risk profile of the MSB by increasing the amount of currency flowing through the MSB.

- Determine if any incomplete or inaccurate documents were filed. Incomplete or inaccurate documents could indicate the MSB does not have appropriate policies and procedures to meet reporting requirements.

- Determine whether there is a history of filing errors that might appear to be systemic.

There are no targeted volumes or "quotas" for SAR-MSB, CTR, CMIR or FBAR filings for a given MSB size or geographic location. Examiners should not criticize an MSB solely because the number of filings is lower than the number filed by "peer" MSBs. However, as part of the examination, examiners should review significant changes in the volume or nature of SAR-MSBs, CTRs, CMIRs, and FBARs filed, and assess potential reasons for these changes.

10. Analyze historical filing trends for reporting requirements. Compare current activity (e.g., number of CTRs, amounts reported on CTRs, types of transactions) to prior examination activity and determine by discussing with management the reason(s) for any significant changes from the prior examination to the current examination.

Risk Assessment

11. Review the MSB's BSA/AML risk assessment. Determine whether the MSB has addressed all risk-related issues, including introduction of any new products or services, customers, agent relationships, other operational risks, geographic locations, etc. Determine whether the MSB's process for periodically reviewing and updating its BSA/AML risk assessment is adequate.

12. If the MSB has not developed a risk assessment, or if the risk assessment is inadequate, complete a risk assessment.

13. Document and discuss the MSB's BSA/AML risk profile and any identified deficiencies in the MSB's BSA/AML risk assessment process with management.

Developing a Risk-Based Examination Plan

14. On the basis of the above examination procedures, and in conjunction with the examiner's review of the MSB's BSA/AML risk assessment, develop an initial examination plan. The examiner should develop an initial examination scope and planning document commensurate with the preliminary BSA/AML risk profile. The examiner should adequately document the plan, as well as any changes to the plan that occur during the examination. Consider the MSB's AML program including policies, procedures, and internal controls to mitigate BSA/AML risks; compliance history; and risk profile (i.e., products, services, customers, geographic locations, etc.). While the examination plan may change at any time as a result of on-site findings, the initial risk assessment will enable the examiner to establish a reasonable scope for the BSA examination. Factors that the examination plan will need to address include:

- The relationship between the MSB's risk assessment and the MSB's AML program's policies and procedures that address those risks. For example, does the MSB have policies and procedures regarding the SAR-MSB reporting requirements that reasonably relate to the MSB's products, services, and customer activities?

- The results of the examiner's review of the MSB's risk assessment or the results of the examiner's risk assessment. High risks require more examination resources. How does the examiner plan to address the BSA/AML risks of the MSB?

- Any differences between the examiner's risk assessment and the MSB's risk assessment.

- Whether the MSB's AML program meets the requirements of the Bank Secrecy Act (the four pillars).

- Potential examination procedures to test the BSA/AML policies and procedures of the MSB. For example, what are the MSB's procedures for filing CTRs? Were the forms timely filed and signed according to the procedures?

- For principal MSB examinations, the compliance responsibilities allocated between the principal MSB and its agents.

The examiner should document in the file any decisions to perform fewer examination procedures for a particular financial service. For example, if the examiner does not devote attention to an MSB's check cashing activities, it may be because the MSB check cashing is a small-volume service where there is a maximum check cashing limit established. Minimal testing can be done in these situations to document the MSB's adherence to its self-imposed limitations.

Transaction Testing Plan

15. Develop a transaction testing plan based on the risk profile of the MSB. The extent of transaction testing and activities conducted should be based on factors that include the examiner's judgment of risks; the MSB's written policies, procedures, and internal controls to mitigate risks; and the adequacy of the independent testing. Note: The adequacy of the independent testing, including the scope of the transaction testing performed during the independent review, should be considered in determining the extent of transaction testing the BSA examiner will do. A BSA examiner may perform minimal transaction testing if the independent review is adequate. Once on-site, the scope of the transaction testing can be adjusted to address any issues or concerns identified during the pre-planning examination stage. The examiner should document any decisions regarding the extent of transaction testing to conduct, the activities for which it is to be performed, and the rationale for any changes to the scope of transaction testing that occur during the examination. Testing should be sufficient to fully assess the degree of risk exposure in a particular function or activity. If the MSB does not have an AML program, or the program is inadequate, then the examiner should perform additional transaction testing procedures (within each section of the manual as applicable to the MSB) to determine the extent, if any, of the MSB's compliance violations.

MSB Registration Requirements — Overview

Objective: *Assess the MSB's compliance with the applicable statutory and regulatory requirements for registration with FinCEN and licensing by the MSB's state licensing authority, if applicable.*

Registration with FinCEN as an MSB is required under certain circumstances if the business is engaged in activities identified in 31 CFR 103.11(uu). The registration should be reviewed in the pre-examination. Certain events require re-registration, which is different from a renewal registration.[19]

Most businesses that meet the definition of an MSB (check cashers; currency dealers or exchangers; money order and traveler's check issuers, sellers, or redeemers; and money transmitters) are required to register using FinCEN Form 107, (formerly TD F90-22.55), Registration of MSB. A person that is an MSB solely because that person serves as an agent of another MSB is not required to register, but an MSB that engages in activities requiring registration on its own behalf must register even if it is also engaging in activities as an agent for others. A branch office of an MSB is not required to file its own registration form. An MSB must, however, report information about its branch locations or offices as provided for in the instructions to the registration form.[20]

An MSB must be registered for the initial registration period and each renewal period. The initial registration period is the two-calendar-year period beginning with the calendar year in which the MSB is first required to be registered. The registration form for the initial registration period must be filed on or before the later of December 31, 2001, or 180 days after the date the business was established or began engaging in MSB activities.

Registration must be renewed every two calendar years beginning with the calendar year in which the initial registration is filed. The registration form for a renewal period must be filed on or before the last day of the calendar year preceding the renewal period (e.g., if the initial registration is filed on November 1, 2007, the renewal must be filed by December 31, 2008, and the next renewal must be filed by December 31, 2010).

Certain events require re-registration of the MSB. Re-registration is different from renewing the registration and is required when:

- An MSB registered or licensed as such under the laws of any state experiences a change in ownership or control that requires the business to re-register or become re-licensed under state law;

---

19. 31 CFR 103.41(b)(4).

20. 31 CFR 103.41.

- The MSB experiences a transfer of more than 10 percent of its voting power or equity interests unless the transfer must be reported to the Securities and Exchange Commission; or

- The MSB experiences a more than 50 percent increase in the number of its agents during any registration period.

The registration form must be filed no later than 180 days after such change in ownership, transfer of voting power or equity interests, or increase in agents. The calendar year in which the change, transfer, or increase occurs is treated as the first year of a new two-year registration period.

Documentation that must be retained includes:

- A copy of the registration form(s) and any registration number that may be assigned to the business;

- Annual estimate of the volume of the registrant's business for the coming year;

- Information regarding ownership or control of the business, including the name and address of any shareholder holding more than five percent of the registrant's stock; the name and address of any general partner; and the name and address of any trustee and/or director or officer of the business; and

- An agent list.

MSBs not required to register include:

- The U.S. Postal Service;

- Agencies of the United States, of any state, or of any political subdivision of a state;

- A person to the extent that the person is an issuer, seller, or redeemer of stored value; and

- A person that is an MSB solely because that person serves as an agent of another MSB or a branch office of an MSB.

MSB Agent List

Certain MSBs must also prepare and maintain a list of their agents.[21] The agent list must be revised each January 1st for the immediately preceding 12 month period and retained for a period of five years. The list is not filed with the registration form but must be maintained at the location in the United States reported on the registration form. Upon request, an MSB must make its list of agents available to FinCEN and any other appropriate law enforcement agency (including, without limitation, the Internal Revenue Service, to which FinCEN has delegated its BSA examination authority).

---

21. 31 CFR 103.41(d).

The agent list must include the following information for each agent:[22]

- The name of the agent, including any trade names or doing-business-as names;

- The address of the agent, including street address, city, state, and ZIP code;

- The telephone number of the agent;

- The type of service or services (money orders, traveler's checks, check sales, check cashing, currency exchange, and money transmitting) the agent provides;

- A listing of those months in the 12 months immediately preceding the date of the most recent agent list in which the gross transaction amount of the agent with respect to financial products or services issued by the MSB maintaining the agent list exceeded $100,000;

- The name and address of any depository institution at which the agent maintains a transaction account (as defined in 12 USC 461(b)(1)(C)) for all or part of the funds received in or for the financial products or services issued by the MSB maintaining the list, whether in the agent's or the business principal's name.

- The year in which the agent first became an agent of the MSB; and

- The number of branches or subagents the agent has.

Note: 31 CFR 103.41 requires the agent list to include the number of branches and sub-agents the agent has; this is also a licensing requirement in certain states.

---

22. 31 CFR 103.41(d)(2).

Examination Procedures
MSB Registration Requirements

1. Verify applicability of the requirement for the MSB to register.

2. Review filed registrations (if applicable) for accuracy and completeness.

   - Review FinCEN form 107, Registration of Money Services Business, and the confirmation from the IRS to ensure accuracy and timely filing.

     - A branch office of an MSB is not required to file its own registration form.

     - An MSB must report information about its branch locations or offices as provided by the instructions to the registration form.

   - Review the supporting documentation for the MSB's registration. A registered MSB must retain:

     - A copy of any registration form filed and any registration number assigned;

     - The annual estimate of the volume of the registrant's business for the coming year;

     - Information regarding ownership or control of the business, including the name and address of any shareholder holding more than five percent of the registrant's stock; the name and address of any general partner; and the name and address of any trustee and/or director or officer of the business; and

     - An agent list (if applicable).

3. Review the agent list (if applicable) for all required elements.

4. Verify the MSB has renewed its registration or re-registered when appropriate as required by 31 CFR 103.41.

On-site Examination and Interview of Appropriate Personnel — Overview

Objective: *Determine whether the MSB has developed, implemented, and administered an effective AML program in accordance with the BSA and implementing regulations.*

Interview

The interviews are critical to conducting a quality BSA examination. Whenever possible, the examiner should conduct at least a portion of the examination at the location of the business. On-site verification of the business activities ensures that the examiner has a thorough understanding of the environment in which the MSB operates and allows the examiner to exercise objective and independent judgment in the performance of the BSA examination.

In-depth interviews of personnel responsible for BSA compliance are key to confirming that the AML program has been effectively implemented. Interviews can provide information on an individual's knowledge of BSA laws and regulations as well as his or her intent and ability to adhere to AML program requirements, as well as BSA reporting, registration, and recordkeeping requirements.

In order to conduct a successful BSA examination, the BSA examiner should have sufficient knowledge of:

- The MSB's organizational structure:
    - History of the MSB and when the financial services were first initiated
    - The structure of the agent/branch providers, where applicable
    - The structure of the foreign counterpart(s) and the MSB's due diligence review of them, where applicable
    - Any anticipated changes to the financial services provided
    - Any issues in the industry or economy that have altered the MSB's business plan;
- Services provided and how these services are conducted. For example:
    - How transmittals of funds are handled, from the initial payment order to the final payment order
    - How services are paid for
    - Average transaction
    - Volume of the services on a yearly basis
    - Risks identified with each of the services provided;

- The MSB's customer base and why the customers use the MSB's service;
- Source and destination of the funds handled by the MSB;
- Type of books and records maintained;
- Procedures developed to ensure compliance with all aspects of the BSA;
- The names and titles of those BSA personnel responsible for compliance and the procedures for which they are responsible; and
- Reporting and communication lines, including who BSA personnel report to and how information is communicated from the top down and vice versa.

Interviews should be conducted from the top down. Upper management and the BSA compliance officer should be the first interviewed as they will set up the background for the MSB's overall knowledge and commitment to BSA compliance. Interviews can then be conducted with supervisory personnel who have been delegated specific managerial review over employees who handle currency transactions and are responsible for filing BSA reports. Interviews should also be conducted with staff who handle day-to-day transactions, as well as agents when the BSA examiner is performing an examination of a principal MSB.

Interviews need to be thorough enough to ensure that the examiner will notice any discrepancies between what the examiner observes in the analysis of the AML program and what the examiner hears from the entity's personnel. The examiner begins to arrive at a preliminary conclusion regarding the effectiveness of the MSB's AML program through the interview process.

In order to effectively and efficiently perform the examination, the examiner should maintain an open line of communication with the MSB whenever possible. The persons responsible for overseeing the day-to-day BSA compliance activities, preparing reports required by the BSA, and obtaining and maintaining records required by the BSA should be questioned regarding their knowledge of BSA recordkeeping and reporting requirements.

The examiner should prepare a Memorandum of Interview relating to each interview conducted during the course of the BSA examination. The examiner should also document additional follow-up questions and relevant conversations in order to support the examiner's final conclusions and subsequent Report of Examination (ROE).

Persons to be interviewed may include the employees, managers, compliance officer, owners, and/or agents where applicable, who:

- Handle currency transactions and money transmissions;
- Are responsible for filing CTRs and SAR-MSBs;
- Review day-to-day BSA compliance; or
- Are responsible for implementing or supervising the AML program.

The examiner should document the responsibilities and duties of BSA personnel. The individual responsible for the implementation of the AML program should be interviewed.

It is extremely important for the BSA examiner to establish and document at the beginning of the BSA compliance examination, the level of BSA knowledge of the MSB owner or directors, compliance officer, managers, and employees, including knowledge of what suspicious activity is, what reporting requirements are, and how to report suspicious activity.

Inquire whether or not appropriate personnel (managers, owners, board members if applicable, etc.,) have knowledge of BSA violations that have not been reported to FinCEN or state regulators.

The interview should identify any related entities. Examiners should ask specific questions relating to the business and services offered. The examiner should consider all financial services or products offered by the business, such as money transmission, check cashing, currency exchange, and sales of money orders/traveler's checks.

For an example of initial interview questions, refer to Appendix G – Sample MSB Interview Questions. This is only a guide that should be modified as each BSA examination warrants.

The answers to the interview questions give the examiner a sense of how the AML program is being implemented. The questions should be tailored to the employee's position and level of responsibility. Not all personnel should be asked the same questions. The compliance officer and those with delegated responsibility for day-to-day oversight should be interviewed as to how various requirements are monitored through various processes, what happens when issues are identified, and their general understanding of the applicable requirements. If those responsible for oversight of the AML program do not understand the requirements applicable to the services offered and relevant to their business function or their own internal policies, there is a possibility that the AML program is not being effectively implemented.

Once the interviews are complete, the examiner should have an understanding of the MSB's AML program, including the policies and procedures as they apply to the BSA/AML risks identified. The next step is for the examiner to consider the types, depth, and scope of internal controls, as well as the transaction monitoring procedures.

Examination Procedures
On-Site Examination and Interview of Appropriate Personnel

1. To the extent not already covered during pre-planning and scoping the examination, interview management and the individual(s) responsible for the AML program. During the interview(s), the examiner should determine and document overall knowledge and commitment to BSA compliance. The interview should also identify any related institutions, branches, and agents. Examiners should ask specific questions relating to the business and services offered. The examiner should consider all financial services or products offered by the business, such as money transmission, check cashing, currency exchange, and sales of money orders/traveler's checks. The interview should document sufficient information to describe the operations of the MSB including:

   - Employees' familiarity with internal compliance programs and internal controls;

   - Independent reviews, including reporting and resolution of findings;

   - Accounts used for money services, including foreign correspondent accounts;

   - Currency controls;

   - On-site records;

   - Off-site records in media other than hard copy;

   - The amount of training received on the BSA recordkeeping and reporting requirements;

   - Reporting requirements;

   - Suspicious activity monitoring requirements; and

   - BSA reporting and recordkeeping requirements, including suspicious activity identification.

2. Interview and document the responsibilities and duties of BSA personnel. During the interview of selected employees, the examiner should determine if the MSB's written AML program has been implemented and operates in the same manner as the described BSA/AML policies and procedures.

3. Ask the appropriate personnel, including agents where applicable, to discuss their process for handling transactions. This may include observation of personnel, including agents where applicable, performing a sample transaction, and having the employee walk you through several types of transactions. Document the process

and evaluate whether the MSB has implemented procedures to ensure compliance with the BSA and evaluate whether processes agree to policies and procedures established by management. The examiner should ascertain and document:

- The types of records maintained;

- Knowledge of currency transaction reporting requirements;

- Where applicable, limits for cashing checks without approval and procedures for cashing large checks;

- Procedures and records maintained for large money orders/traveler's checks sold;

- Procedures for preparing CTRs and SAR-MSBs;

- Procedures for obtaining records required for transmittals of funds; and

- Procedures for obtaining records required for currency exchange or dealing.

4. Interview employees of the MSB, including front line employees, owners, management, and agents where applicable, as to whether or not they have knowledge (appropriate to their responsibilities) of what constitutes suspicious activity and what the reporting requirements are for suspicious activity.

For an example of initial interview questions, refer to Appendix G – Sample MSB Interview Questions. This is only a guide that should be modified as each BSA examination warrants.

Anti-Money Laundering Program — Overview

Objective: *Assess the adequacy of the MSB's anti-money laundering program. Determine whether the MSB has developed, administered, and maintained an effective risk-based program for compliance with the BSA and all of its implementing regulations.*

MSBs are required by 31 CFR 103.125 to implement an effective anti-money laundering (AML) program that is reasonably designed to prevent the MSB from being used to facilitate money laundering and terrorist financing. The anti-money laundering program must be written and must be commensurate with the MSB's risk profile. Furthermore, the program must be fully implemented and reasonably designed to meet the BSA requirements. Policy statements alone are not sufficient; practices must coincide with the MSB's written program.

Federal regulators have the authority to request the written AML program of the MSB.[23] The authority of states to regulate MSBs varies by state, from no requirements specified in regulations to extensive recordkeeping and safety and soundness requirements. The examiner should test the elements of the MSB's AML program to determine whether the program is adequate.

MSBs that have automated data processing systems should integrate such systems into their compliance procedures. In addition, an MSB that is an MSB solely because it is an agent for another MSB may, by agreement with the MSB for which it serves as agent, allocate between itself and that MSB the responsibility for developing policies, procedures, and internal controls required by the BSA.[24] Both the principal and the agent remain independently responsible for implementation of the requirements of the BSA, and nothing in 31 CFR 103.125 relieves any MSB from its obligations to establish and maintain an effective AML program.

Strong management commitment to the anti-money laundering program promotes ongoing compliance and helps prevent the MSB from being used to launder money or facilitate terrorist financing.

Where possible, the AML program should be obtained and reviewed prior to the on-site portion of the examination. This will assist the examiner in determining the risk profile of the MSB and the scope of the examination.

---

23. 31 CFR 103.125(c).
24. 31 CFR 103.125(d)(1)(iii).

Developing a Risk-Based AML program – The Four Pillars

Management should understand the MSB's BSA/AML risk exposure and develop appropriate policies, procedures, and processes to monitor and control BSA/AML risks. For those MSBs that have a higher BSA/AML risk profile, management should provide a more robust program that specifically identifies, monitors, and controls the higher risks that management has accepted. An effective risk assessment should be an ongoing process, not a one-time exercise. Management should update its risk assessment to identify changes in the MSB's risk profile as necessary (e.g., when new products and services are introduced, existing products and services change, the MSB targets new customer markets, or the MSB expands operations) and make appropriate changes to the AML program. At a minimum, the MSB's AML program must include the following four pillars:

- Policies, procedures, and internal controls designed to ensure ongoing compliance;

- Designation of individual(s) responsible for coordinating and monitoring day-to-day compliance;

- Training for appropriate personnel; and

- Independent review to monitor an adequate program.

1. Internal Controls

Internal controls are the MSB's policies, procedures, and processes designed to detect, prevent, limit, and control money laundering and terrorist financing risks. Internal controls include policies, procedures, and processes for detecting and reporting required transactions and activity. It is important for MSB management to create a culture of compliance to ensure staff adherence to the MSB's AML program. The level of sophistication of the internal controls should be commensurate with the size, structure, risks, and complexity of the MSB. Internal controls should provide for:

- Effective risk assessment, including periodic updates to the MSB's risk profile;

- Development and implementation of policies, procedures, and internal controls to ensure compliance with all applicable BSA requirements and mitigation of risks identified by risk assessment;

- Verification of customer identity;

- Filing of required reports;

- Creation and maintenance of required records;

- Responding to law enforcement requests; and

- Integration of automated data processing systems into BSA compliance.

A system of internal controls must be in place that is reasonably designed to ensure compliance with the BSA. The AML program should provide for these procedures and set forth the policies, procedures, and internal controls that the MSB will adhere to in the conduct of its operations. Many of the areas discussed in this section will probably not be present in smaller operations. However, the general principle that the MSB should have some type of internal controls to mitigate risk applies to all MSBs, regardless of size.

Generally, a system of internal controls can be evaluated from the following perspectives:

A. Risk Assessment

B. Control Environment

C. Internal Control Activities

D. Information and Communications

E. Internal Control Monitoring

F. Responding to Law Enforcement Inquiries and Requests

G. Principal MSB Monitoring/Oversight Procedures

H. Requirements for MSBs with Respect to Foreign Agents or Foreign Counterparties

Large complex MSBs are more likely to implement departmental internal controls for BSA compliance. Departmental internal controls typically address risks and compliance requirements unique to a particular line of business or department and are part of a comprehensive AML program. These departmental internal controls could be contained in a desk guide or some other similar document that describes the duties for each BSA position.

The BSA examiner should develop a thorough understanding of the financial services offered and books and records maintained by the entity. From this overview of how business is conducted, the business practices utilized by the MSB should become clearer.

The BSA examiner needs to develop an understanding of the internal controls of the MSB. This understanding should include an identification of what the MSB's policies, practices, and procedures to prevent, detect, and limit the risks are that an MSB could be used to launder money or facilitate terrorist financing activities. The examiner also needs to determine whether those controls are in place and functioning as described. The best way to test internal controls is by walking through the MSB's procedures and transaction processing. The MSB should be able to show the examiner how a transaction is performed by walking the examiner through the process. This should include all manual and automated systems. An examiner will test the records of the MSB and document the effectiveness of the MSB's internal controls.

A. Management's Risk Assessment

Management should structure the MSB's AML program to adequately address the risks identified by management's risk assessment. Management should understand the MSB's risk exposure and develop the appropriate policies, procedures, and processes to monitor and control BSA/AML risks. For example, the MSB's monitoring systems to identify, research, and report suspicious activity should be risk-based, with particular emphasis on high-risk products, services, customers, geographic locations, etc. as identified by the MSB's risk assessment.

Various factors can be considered in analyzing an MSB's risk assessment. This list is not comprehensive, but instead provides a starting point:

- What financial services does the MSB offer? Do those financial services involve unique risks? What is the sales volume of those activities? For an MSB acting solely as an agent of a principal MSB, standard BSA/AML procedures created by the principal MSB (e.g., an agent engaging in the sale of money orders for a principal MSB) could adequately address these risks or may need to be modified to address the unique circumstances of the agent MSB.

- Does the MSB management perform a risk assessment?

- If MSB management does perform a risk assessment, how is risk identified, ranked, analyzed, mitigated, and communicated to the appropriate staff?

- Does MSB management have mechanisms in place to identify risks to the MSB from changes in its business environment, such as changes in its customer base or technological advancements and developments?

- Does MSB management consider the risks associated with employee and management turnover and the potential impact on BSA compliance?

- Are there any mechanisms in place to anticipate, identify, and react to risks presented by changes in BSA regulations or other conditions that can affect BSA compliance?

MSB's Updating of the Risk Assessment

An effective AML program controls risks associated with the MSB's products, services, customers, agent relationships, operations, geographic locations etc; therefore, an effective risk assessment should be an ongoing process, not a one-time exercise. Management should update its risk assessment to identify changes in the MSB's risk profile as necessary (e.g., prior to introducing new products and services, changing existing products and services, or MSB expansion through mergers and acquisitions). Even in the absence of such changes, it is a sound practice for MSBs to periodically reassess the BSA/AML risks of the MSB.

Performing a risk assessment is also discussed in detail in the Pre-Planning Section Overview.

B. Control Environment

The control environment for an MSB can be evidenced by the conscientiousness of management in adhering to BSA regulations. During the BSA examination, determine if the entity has taken steps to ensure BSA compliance and made consistent efforts to ensure employees' adherence to BSA regulations. Alternatively, did management merely document the requirements with little or no regard to actual BSA compliance and AML program implementation? Were employees aware of the various reporting requirements, and did they follow the policies and procedures of the MSB to ensure compliance? All of these factors can provide an indicator as to whether an entity is committed to BSA compliance.

Various factors can be considered in analyzing an MSB's control environment. This list is not comprehensive, but instead provides a starting point in the internal control analysis:

- Do the employees know their responsibilities as outlined in the entity's AML program?
- Do the employees know the BSA reporting requirements and other related sections of the BSA?
- Do the employees periodically review these requirements?
- When employee questions arise regarding BSA requirements and responsibilities, does MSB management address them timely?
- Is the MSB management cooperative with auditors, examiners, and BSA compliance officers?
- Does MSB management take prompt remedial action when potential errors or problems have been identified?
- How does MSB management address improper intervention or overriding of internal control procedures and policies?
- How does MSB management respond to independent review findings?
- Has appropriate training been provided to employees?
- Is the training updated and provided to employees periodically?

C. Internal Control Activities

Internal control activities are policies, procedures, techniques, and mechanisms that assist management in ensuring that the risks of BSA non-compliance identified during the risk assessment process are mitigated. Internal control activities are essential for achieving BSA compliance and should be a primary focus of the planning, implementation, and review of the AML program. Internal control activities will vary depending on the size of the MSB as well as the products and services offered. Some examples of control activities that could be in place include: computer programs in a point-of-sale system that require all fields to be completed; error recognition in these programs if invalid data is entered; dollar limits on transactions that will be processed without a manager's approval; systems that automatically prompt an employee to obtain additional recordkeeping information when applicable; and clear instructions on types of customer identification that will be accepted as proof of identity.

Various factors can be considered in examining an MSB's internal control activities. This list is not comprehensive, but instead provides a starting point for analyzing the effectiveness of those activities:

- Do the internal control activities that are in place address the risks identified in management's risk assessment? For example, if an MSB cashes checks that exceed $10,000, have processes been implemented to review check cashing activity and ensure that CTRs are being filed when required?

- Are the control activities periodically evaluated to determine if they are still appropriate and working as intended? For example, if the MSB's processing system automatically prompts an employee to obtain additional recordkeeping information for sales of money orders/traveler's checks of $3,000 or more, have the control activities been tested to ensure they are working appropriately?

- Is there a reporting process to ensure that management is provided periodic updates on BSA compliance within the MSB?

- What procedures are in place to ensure that personnel hired have the appropriate skills to perform their jobs?

- How does management respond when a transaction is conducted outside of the control environment?

- How does management respond when control activities do not prevent the processing of a transaction that should not have been processed?

- For MSBs that maintain computers for transactional processing — are there back-up systems? If so, how are the systems maintained and information safeguarded?

- For MSBs that maintain computers for transactional processing — how is access to the systems controlled?

- How is documentation covering the internal control structure of the business maintained? Is it readily available for review? Is it updated as necessary?

D. Information and Communications

The information and communications maintained by the MSB regarding its compliance efforts and transactional documentation must be relevant and reliable. Various factors can be considered in analyzing an MSB's information and communications processes. This list is not comprehensive, but instead provides a starting point for analyzing the effectiveness of an MSB's information and communications processes:

- In order to comply with specific BSA recordkeeping requirements, has the MSB identified and implemented policies and procedures to ensure that the required records are properly prepared and maintained? Can the records be retrieved when necessary?

- Does management keep employees apprised of internal procedural changes as well as any changes in regulations that could affect their duties?

- Has the MSB clearly assigned BSA duties and responsibilities to the appropriate employees and communicated those assignments? Do the MSB's employees understand the relevant aspects of internal controls and how their work relates to internal control and the work of others?

- Do employees know what steps to take in the event of unusual transactions?

- If employees identify a weakness in internal control procedures or policies, is there a means of communicating this information to management?

- If an entity uses a computer system, is this system monitored, analyzed, and evaluated to ensure reliability?

E. Internal Control Monitoring

The purposes of internal control monitoring are to assess the performance quality of the MSB's internal control systems over time and to ensure that independent review, examination, and other findings are promptly resolved. This monitoring includes regular management and supervisory activities. Other tools can be utilized in this monitoring including self-assessments, control design review, and direct testing.

Below are various factors that can be considered in analyzing an MSB's internal control monitoring. This list is not comprehensive, but instead provides a starting point for analyzing the effectiveness of an MSB's internal control monitoring:

- Has the MSB implemented internal controls? Are its internal controls operating correctly?

- Are internal control responsibilities taken seriously by management and is the importance of these procedures communicated to employees?

- Does management receive routine feedback on the monitoring of internal control systems? How does management correct errors and deficiencies?

- How does the MSB monitor its day-to-day activities?

- Who is responsible for correcting any deficiencies identified in the internal control systems?

- Who is responsible for ensuring that independent review, examination, or other findings are resolved?

An entity that is an MSB solely because it is an agent for a principal may allocate the responsibility for development of policies, procedures, and internal controls required by the BSA between itself and its principal by agreement with the principal. Even if such an agreement exists, 31 CFR 103.125(d)(1) does not relieve an MSB from its obligations to establish and maintain an effective AML program. Each MSB remains solely responsible for its own compliance with the requirements of the BSA.

F. Responding to Law Enforcement Inquiries and Requests

MSBs should establish policies, procedures, and processes for responding to law enforcement inquiries and requests. Law enforcement inquiries and requests can include grand jury subpoenas and National Security Letters (NSLs). Policies, procedures, and processes should ensure such inquiries and requests are handled appropriately. For example, an MSB may establish procedures under which all requests go through a central location in order to ensure that requests are handled timely and appropriately. Procedures may also include identifying subjects of law enforcement requests, monitoring the transaction activity of those subjects, identifying unusual or suspicious activity related to those subjects, and filing SAR-MSBs related to those subjects if warranted.

G. Principal MSB Monitoring/Oversight Procedures

Principal MSBs may offer financial services through either branches or agents. One of the major risk exposures of a principal MSB is that one of its branches or agents will engage in transactions that put both the branch/agent and the principal at risk for money laundering or other financial crimes. In order to reduce this risk, the principal MSB should have procedures in place to identify those branches/agents that conduct transactions that appear to lack commercial justification or otherwise cannot be supported by verifiable documentation.

Once high risk branches/agents are identified, the principal MSB should implement procedures to ensure that the transactions those branches/agents conduct are legitimate. The procedures should also ensure that, if transactions at those branches/agents trigger reporting or recordkeeping requirements, the information has been obtained and retained.

In addition, the principal MSB should implement procedures for handling non-compliance at branches/agents (e.g., agent contract termination).

H. Requirements for MSBs with Respect to Foreign Agents or Foreign Counterparties

Interpretive guidance on handling foreign agents and foreign counterparties was issued by FinCEN on December 14, 2004.[25] This guidance clarifies that MSBs are required to establish adequate and appropriate policies, procedures, and controls commensurate with the risks of money laundering and the financing of terrorism posed by their relationship with foreign agents or foreign counterparties of the MSB. The focus of the interpretive guidance was the establishment and maintenance of the relationship between an MSB and its foreign agent or foreign counterparty that facilitates the flow of funds into and out of the United States on behalf of customers.

With respect to MSBs that utilize foreign agents or counterparties to facilitate the movement of funds into or out of the US, an MSB's AML program must include risk-based policies, procedures, and internal controls designed to identify and minimize money laundering and terrorist financing risks associated with foreign agents and counterparties. The AML program must be aimed at preventing the products and services of the MSB from being used to facilitate money laundering or terrorist financing through these relationships, and at detecting the use of these products and services for money laundering or terrorist financing by the MSB or agents. Relevant risk factors may include, but are not limited to:

- Location and jurisdiction of the foreign agent or counterparty. This would include considering the extent to which the relevant jurisdiction is internationally recognized as presenting a greater risk for money laundering, or is considered to have more robust AML standards;

- Ownership of the foreign agent or counterparty. This includes whether the owners are known, upon reasonable inquiry, to be associated with criminal conduct or terrorism;

- The extent to which the foreign agent or counterparty is subject to AML requirements in its jurisdiction and whether it has established AML controls;

- Information known or readily available to the MSB about the foreign agent or counterparty's AML record, including public record;

- The nature of the foreign agent or counterparty's business, the markets it serves, and the extent to which its business and markets served present increased exposure to money laundering or terrorist financing;

- Types and purpose of services to be provided to, and anticipated activity with, the foreign agent or counterparty; and

- Nature and duration of the relationship between the MSB and its foreign agent or counterparty.

---

25. See Appendix H.

The MSB's AML program should include procedures for the following:

- Conduct due diligence on foreign agents and counterparties;
- Risk-based monitoring of foreign agents or counterparties; and
- Corrective actions and termination.

2. Designation of BSA Compliance Officer

The MSB must designate a qualified individual to serve as the BSA compliance officer. The BSA compliance officer is responsible for coordinating and ensuring day-to-day BSA compliance. The BSA compliance officer is also responsible for assuring that:

- The MSB properly files reports and creates and maintains records in accordance with the requirements of the BSA;
- The AML program is updated as necessary to reflect current BSA requirements and related guidance; and
- The MSB provides appropriate training and education to applicable staff.

While the title of the individual responsible for overall BSA compliance is not important, his or her level of authority and responsibility within the MSB is critical. The BSA compliance officer may delegate specific duties to other employees, but the officer is responsible for overall BSA compliance. The BSA compliance officer should be fully knowledgeable about the BSA and all related regulations. The BSA compliance officer should also understand the MSB's products, services, customers, geographic locations, etc., as well as the potential money laundering and terrorist financing risks associated with those activities. The designation of a BSA compliance officer is not sufficient to meet the regulatory requirement if that person does not have the expertise, authority, or resources to satisfactorily complete the job.

3. Independent Review

The AML program must provide for an independent review of the program in order to assess effectiveness. Because the independent review need not be a formal audit by a certified public accountant or third-party consultant, an MSB does not necessarily need to hire an outside auditor or consultant. An officer, employee or group of employees may conduct the review, so long as none of the reviewers are the designated BSA compliance officer or reports directly to the BSA compliance officer.

The primary purpose of the independent review is to determine the adequacy of the MSB's AML program, including whether the business is operating in compliance with the requirements of the Bank Secrecy Act and the MSB's own policies and procedures.

The review should provide a fair and unbiased appraisal of each of the required elements of the MSB's AML program, including its Bank Secrecy Act-related policies, procedures, internal controls, recordkeeping and reporting functions, and training. The review should be based on the risks to the MSB, should test the MSB's risk assessment for reasonableness and should determine the adequacy of the risk mitigation strategies chosen by the MSB. The review should include testing of internal controls and transactional systems and procedures to identify problems and weaknesses and, if necessary, recommend to management appropriate corrective actions. For example, if the program requires that a particular employee or category of employee should be trained once every six months, then the independent testing should determine whether the training occurred and whether the training was adequate. The review should include transactional testing to determine if all requirements of the MSB's AML program have been implemented and if policies, procedures, processes, and internal controls are working appropriately. Where applicable the review should include the principal MSB's policies, procedures, and processes for agent relationships, including how the MSB maintains oversight over agents related to BSA compliance. This includes establishing new agent relationships, monitoring existing relationships, and handling non-compliance by agents, including termination of agent relationships where appropriate.

The review also should cover all of the AML program actions taken by – or defined as part of the responsibility of – the designated BSA compliance officer. These actions include, for example, the determination of the level of money laundering risk faced by the business, the frequency of BSA/AML training for employees, and the adoption of procedures for implementation and oversight of program-related controls and transactional systems.

Timing of the Independent Review

The review should be conducted on a periodic basis. The scope and frequency of the review will depend on the MSB's risk assessment, which should take into account the MSB's products, services, customers, geographic locations, etc. For some MSBs, based on their risk assessments, an annual review may not be necessary; for others, more frequent review may be warranted. For example, if the MSB's risk assessment changes, more frequent review may be prudent. Similarly, if compliance problems are identified in a review, it may be advisable to advance the date of the next review to confirm that corrective actions have been taken.

Documentation and Follow-Up

The person or persons responsible for conducting the review should document the scope of the review, procedures performed, transaction testing completed, if any, findings of the review, and recommendations to management for corrective actions, if any. After the review, the reviewer or the designated BSA compliance officer should track deficiencies and weaknesses discovered during the review and document corrective actions taken by the MSB. All of the documentation should, as appropriate, be made accessible to government examiners and law enforcement personnel who have authority to examine such documents.

4. Training

MSBs must ensure that appropriate personnel are trained in applicable aspects of the BSA and their own responsibilities under the MSB's AML program. To the extent that regulations require MSBs to file Suspicious Activity Reports, the program must also provide for training in the detection of suspicious transactions to appropriate personnel.

At a minimum, the MSB's training program must provide training for all personnel whose duties require knowledge of the BSA. The training should be tailored to the employee's specific responsibilities. In addition, an overview of the BSA requirements typically should be given to new staff during employee orientation.

Training should be ongoing and should incorporate current developments and changes to the BSA and any related regulations. Changes to internal policies, procedures, processes, and monitoring systems should also be covered during training. Training should reinforce the importance that management places on compliance with the BSA and should ensure that all employees understand their role in maintaining an effective AML program.

Examples of money laundering activity and suspicious activity monitoring and reporting can and should be tailored to each individual audience. Training and testing materials, the dates of training sessions, and attendance records should be maintained by the MSB and be available for examiner review.

Examniation Procedures
Anti-Money Laundering Program

1. Review the MSB's written AML program to ensure it contains the following required elements:
   - Policies, procedures, and internal controls designed to ensure ongoing compliance;
   - Designation of individual(s) responsible for coordinating and monitoring day-to-day compliance;
   - Training for appropriate personnel; and
   - Independent review to adequately monitor program.

Risk Assessment

2. Based on examination procedures completed during scoping and planning, including the review of the risk assessment, determine whether the MSB has adequately assessed its risks and incorporated them into the MSB's AML program. (Refer also to the Pre-Planning the BSA Examination - Overview and Pre-Planning the BSA Examination - Examination Procedures sections of this manual for additional information.)

Internal Controls

3. Develop a thorough understanding of the MSB's policies, procedures, and processes designed to ensure compliance with the BSA. This review should be completed prior to starting any transactional testing. An MSB's AML program must be commensurate with its BSA/AML risk profile. Determine if policies, procedures, and processes:
   - Provide for program continuity despite changes in management or employee composition or structure;
   - Meet all regulatory requirements, address recommendations for BSA compliance, and provide for timely updates to changes in regulations;
   - Provide for the identification of reportable transactions and the accurate filing of all required reports, including SAR-MSBs and CTRs;
   - Provide sufficient controls and monitoring systems for the timely detection and reporting of suspicious activities;
   - Provide for adequate supervision of employees that handle currency transactions, complete reports, monitor for suspicious activities, or engage in any other activity covered by the BSA and its implementing regulations;

- Address the BSA/AML risks identified in the examiner's and/or the MSB's risk assessment;

- Provide for collecting and verifying customer identification. Determine through review of documents and discussion whether there are adequate and effective policies and procedures for verifying customer identification as appropriate;

- Provide for creating and retaining records. Does the MSB have processes to ensure required information is obtained and retained for the required timeframe? Is there a review process to ensure adequate records are being obtained? and

- Provide for responding to law enforcement requests. Does the MSB have a process for handling law enforcement requests? Are the appropriate personnel involved in the process? For example, do all requests go through the BSA compliance officer?

4. Identify and document the transaction cycle of the products and services of the MSB through discussion and observation. This process should answer the Who, What, Where, and Why of the MSB's activities so the examiner can evaluate the appropriateness of risk-based internal controls, policies, and procedures implemented by the MSB.

5. Identify, document, analyze, and evaluate the day-to-day system of monitoring transactions for BSA reporting requirements. Determine whether monitoring systems are appropriate based on the risks of the MSB.

6. Determine if senior management or the board of directors, where applicable, is provided adequate reports on anti-money laundering and BSA compliance. Perform an assessment of personnel efforts regarding communicating with senior management or the board of directors, where applicable, on issues of anti-money laundering.

- Where applicable, determine if reports are provided to the board of directors or an established compliance committee. If so, review the minutes to ensure discussions have been documented.

- Obtain a copy of all reports that were provided to management or the board of directors, where applicable, regarding BSA compliance during the review period.

- Determine if personnel are providing sufficient information to senior management or the board of directors (where applicable) to ensure BSA compliance is adequately addressed.

Principal MSB Monitoring/Oversight Procedures

7. Review the principal MSB's policies and procedures for monitoring/oversight of branches and agents. Determine through interviews, assessment of the principal MSB's risk, and analysis of the principal MSB's policies, procedures, and internal controls whether policies, procedures, and internal controls are adequate.

8. Identify those branches/agents that are at highest risk. Factors to consider should not be based solely on the total volume of the various financial services offered. An agent that conducts $500,000 in funds transmittals in a month is not in itself high risk. However, if the majority of the transactions are conducted at or right below the identification requirements or self-imposed limitations, then those factors put the branch/agent at a higher risk than an agent that has the same volume but with a majority of transactions at much smaller amounts. Those branches/agents that have a higher risk for recordkeeping and reporting requirement violations may also be at higher risk for potential suspicious activity occurring. Ensure that the principal MSB has identified its high risk branches/agents and has appropriately monitored associated transactions.

9. Examine a sample of the higher risk branches/agents to determine their BSA compliance and whether the branches/agents have had any contact with the principal MSB relative to compliance requirements, including training on recordkeeping as well as identification and filing reports, such as suspicious activity reports. Determine if branches/agents have received adequate BSA/AML training.

10. If a principal MSB files SAR-MSBs for agents, the examiner should determine what type of contact is made with the agent MSB to ensure its employees understand the requirements.

11. Review files of those agents whose contracts have been terminated by the principal MSB to determine why they no longer offer the principal MSB's financial services. It is possible that the agent has gone to another service provider and follow-up may be warranted on those agents.

12. For branches, ascertain the branches' BSA knowledge, areas of noncompliance and any corrective action documented by the branches. Examiners need to identify whether the headquarters is aware of any issues raised at the branch level related to BSA compliance and any corrective action implemented. (The principal MSB headquarters is ultimately responsible for the compliance of all its branches.)

Additional Examination Procedure for Branch/Agent Monitoring/ Oversight Based on Risk

13. Review a sample of SAR-MSBs filed by the agent MSB location where transactions were conducted. SAR-MSBs filed on transactions conducted at an agent location should be reviewed to determine whether the agent MSB's procedures for reporting are appropriate. Determine whether the principal MSB maintains appropriate communication and oversight of agent MSB SAR-MSB filing activity where appropriate.

Requirement for MSBs with Respect to Foreign Agents or Foreign Counterparties

14. Ensure that the MSB's AML program establishes procedures for conducting reasonable, risk-based due diligence on potential and existing foreign agents and counterparties to help ensure that such foreign agents and counterparties are not

themselves complicit in illegal activity involving the MSBs products and services, and that the foreign agent or foreign counterparty have appropriate AML controls in place to guard against the abuse of the MSB's products and services. Due diligence must, at a minimum, include:

- Reasonable procedures to identify the owners of the MSB's foreign agents and counterparties;

- Procedures to evaluate, on an ongoing basis, the operations of those foreign agents and counterparties and their implementation of policies, procedures, and controls reasonably designed to help assure that the MSB's products and services are not subject to abuse by the foreign agent's or counterparty's customers, employees, or contractors;

- Procedures to review location and jurisdiction of the MSB's foreign agents/ counterparties. Consider the nature of the business of the foreign agents/ counterparties, the markets they serve, and the extent to which these increase their risk for money laundering or terrorist activity; and

- Evaluation of the types and purpose of service to be provided and anticipated activity with the foreign agents/counterparties.

15. Ensure that the MSB has established procedures for risk-based monitoring and review of transactions from, to, or through the United States that are conducted through foreign agents and counterparties. Such procedures should also focus on identifying material changes in the agent's risk profile, such as change in ownership, business, or the regulatory scrutiny to which it is subject. In addition, MSBs should have procedures in place to enable them to review foreign agent or counterparty activity for signs of structuring or unnecessarily complex transmissions through multiple jurisdictions that may be indicative of layering.

16. Review the MSB's procedures for responding to foreign agents or counterparties that present unreasonable risks of money laundering. Such procedures should provide for the implementation of corrective action on the part of the foreign agents or counterparties or the termination of relationships with the foreign agents or counterparties that pose an unacceptable risk of money laundering or terrorist financing, or that demonstrate systemic, willful, or repeated lapses in compliance with the MSB's own AML procedures or requirements.

17. For currency dealers or exchangers, review the bank records for all the domestic and foreign bank accounts over which the currency dealer or exchanger has authority. Many currency dealers or exchangers have foreign bank accounts or use foreign bank accounts held in agent or nominee names to facilitate conducting their financial services. The examiner should ask for foreign bank account records.

18. Analyze the volume and size of transactions being conducted at each foreign agent/ counterparty.

- Identify patterns of significant changes. Review the agent files for those with significant changes.

- Identify agents in jurisdictions where their AML program requirements may be weaker.

- Identify agents in locations where it is known that illegal activity such as drug trafficking is common.

- Review activity for signs of structuring or unnecessarily complex transmissions through multiple jurisdictions that may be indicative of layering.

- Review the MSB's response to agents conducting transactions that place them at a higher risk.

BSA Compliance Officer

19. Determine whether the BSA compliance officer has the necessary authority and resources to effectively execute all duties. The BSA compliance officer should have adequate involvement in development and implementation of new policies, processes, services, products, agents, etc. There should also be an adequate reporting line for compliance matters.

20. Determine if the BSA compliance officer's education, training, and experience are adequate for the duties and responsibilities defined in his/her job description.

21. Assess the competency of the BSA compliance officer and his or her staff, as necessary. Determine whether the BSA compliance area is sufficiently staffed for the MSB's overall risk level (based on products, services, customers, geographic locations, etc.), size, and BSA compliance needs. In addition, ensure that no conflict of interest exists and that staff is given adequate time to execute all duties.

Independent Testing

22. Determine whether the BSA/AML testing is independent (i.e.., performed by a person or persons who do not include the BSA compliance officer, a person reporting directly to the compliance officer, or a person involved in funds transactions, etc.). The person(s) performing the independent testing should not be involved in the development or revision of the AML program, policies, procedures, and training.

23. Evaluate the qualifications of the person(s) performing the independent testing to assess whether the MSB can rely upon the findings and conclusions.

24. Review the reports and workpapers from the independent testing to determine whether it is comprehensive, accurate, adequate, and timely. The independent testing should address the following:

- The overall integrity and effectiveness of the AML program, including policies, procedures, and processes;

- BSA/AML risk assessment;

- BSA reporting and recordkeeping requirements;

- Personnel adherence to the MSB's BSA/AML policies, procedures, and processes;

- Appropriate transaction testing, with particular emphasis on high-risk areas;

- Adequacy of training, including comprehensiveness, accuracy of materials, the training schedule, and attendance tracking;

- The integrity and accuracy of management information systems (MIS) used in the AML program (e.g., whether MIS includes reports that identify large currency transactions, aggregate daily currency transactions, monitor transmittals of funds, and money order or traveler's checks sales transactions); and

- Agent oversight, where applicable.

25. Review the scope, procedures, and workpapers to determine adequacy of the independent testing based on the following:

- Overall testing coverage and frequency in relation to the risk profile of the MSB;

- Management's reporting and supervision of, and its responsiveness to, testing findings;

- Adequacy of transaction testing, particularly for high-risk operations and suspicious activity monitoring systems. Ensure the independent review tested the validity and accuracy of the transaction identification system utilized by the MSB. If an automated or large transaction identification or aggregation system is not used, did the review test transactions conducted by the MSB for the examination period to determine if large transactions are being reported? and

- Competency of the independent reviewers regarding BSA requirements.

Note: The adequacy of the independent testing, including the scope of the transaction testing performed during the independent review, should be considered in determining the extent of transaction testing the BSA examiner will do. A BSA examiner may perform minimal transaction testing if the independent review is adequate.

Training

26. Determine whether the MSB's training program and materials adequately address the following elements:

- The importance management and the board of directors, where applicable, place on ongoing education, training, and compliance;

- Employee accountability for ensuring BSA compliance;

- Comprehensiveness of training, considering specific risks of individual business lines;

- Training of appropriate personnel from all applicable areas of the MSB;

- Frequency of training;

- Documentation of attendance records and training materials;

- Coverage of the MSB's policies, procedures, and processes;

- Coverage of different forms of money laundering and terrorist financing as this information relates to identification and examples of suspicious activities; and

- Incorporation of new and revised changes to the BSA and related regulations.

27. Engage in discussions with appropriate employees to assess their knowledge of BSA/AML policies and regulatory requirements.

28. Determine whether management's procedures are appropriate to ensure all applicable personnel receive training. As appropriate, review employee training records to determine whether all appropriate personnel have received training.

Preliminary Evaluation

29. After the examiner has completed the review of all required elements of the MSB's overall AML program, the examiner should document a preliminary evaluation of the MSB's program. At this point, the examiner should revisit the initial examination plan, in order to determine whether any strengths or weaknesses identified during the review of the MSB's AML program warrant adjustments to the initial planned scope. The examiner should document and explain any changes to the examination scope.

Recordkeeping Requirements — Overview

Objective: *Assess the adequacy of the MSB's anti-money laundering recordkeeping. Determine whether the MSB maintains required records and documents to administer an effective risk-based program for compliance with the BSA and all of its implementing regulations.*

The next phase of a BSA examination is the examination of the records and transactions of the MSB, including financial and accounting records, third-party records such as bank statements and customer invoices, and other source documents to support the BSA recordkeeping requirements and accounting records.

Recordkeeping Requirements

31 CFR 103 has numerous sections on recordkeeping requirements. Recordkeeping requirements for a transaction depend on the type of business making the record, the type of transaction, and the amount of the transaction. In some cases, the information to be recorded must be verified and the document used to verify the information must be described in the record. Typical business records may be used in the verification process. If no record is made in the ordinary course of business of any transaction with respect to which records are required to be retained by 31 CFR 103.38, then such a record shall be prepared in writing by the MSB.[26] MSBs must create or maintain records when required by a special targeting order.[27] Records for agent MSBs may be maintained by the principal MSB.

All MSBs are required to keep records on extensions of credit over $10,000 and instructions regarding transfers over $10,000 into or out of the United States.[28]

Records to be Maintained for Issuance or Sale of Money Orders/Traveler's Checks

An MSB must maintain a record of the issuance or sale of a cashier's check, money order, or traveler's check for $3,000 or more in currency.[29] Federal regulations do not require a specific format for these records. 31 CFR 103.29(a)(2) requires an MSB not

---

26. 31 CFR 103.38(b).
27. 31 CFR 103.26.
28. 31 CFR 103.33.
29. 31 CFR 103.29.

to issue or sell a cashier's check, money order, or traveler's check for $3,000 or more in currency unless it maintains records of specific information. This information must be obtained for each issuance or sale of one or more instruments to any individual purchaser that involves currency in the amount of $3,000 to $10,000, inclusive, by or on behalf of one individual in one business day.[30] The following information must be obtained for the records of such issuance or sale:

- The purchaser's name and address. The MSB is required to verify the purchaser's name and address and record the specific identifying information (e.g., state of issuance and purchaser's driver's license number). When the purchaser is not an account holder, the MSB shall verify the purchaser's name and address by examination of a document that is normally acceptable within the banking community as a means of identification when cashing checks and that contains the name and address of the purchaser, and shall record the specific identifying information (e.g., state of issuance and number of driver's license)[31] ;

- The date of purchase;

- The type of instruments purchased;

- The serial numbers of the instruments purchased;

- The amount in dollars of each instrument purchased;

- When the purchaser is not an account holder, the purchaser's social security number or alien identification number; and

- When the purchaser is not an account holder, the purchaser's date of birth.

Contemporaneous purchases of the same or different types of instruments totaling $3,000 or more are treated as one purchase if an employee, officer, or partner of the MSB has knowledge that the purchases have occurred.

Records to be Maintained for Transmittals of Funds

A record of transmittals of funds must be maintained.[32]   31 CFR 103.33(f) requires each MSB agent, agency, branch, or office located within the United States to obtain and retain information relating to the transmittal of funds in the amount of $3,000 or more. Principal MSBs may maintain centralized records for its agents. Note: For transmittals greater than $10,000 made with currency, the information maintained under this section is required in addition to a CTR.

---

30. 31 CFR 103.29(a).

31. 31 CFR 103.29(a)(2)(ii).

32. 31 CFR 103.33.

An MSB must keep either the original, microfilm, other copy, or reproduction of each transaction that results (or is intended to result) in the transfer of more than $10,000 in currency or monetary instruments to or from any person, account, or place outside the United States.[33]

Note: There is no aggregation rule for transmittals to reach the $3,000 limit requirement to secure the additional identification information.[34]

Certain records are required to be retained for transmittals of $3,000 or more sent or received by or for an individual on any one business day.[35] If a sender is an established customer, the following records must be retained:

- The sender's name and address;
- The amount of the transmittal order;
- The execution date of the transmittal order;
- Any payment instructions received from the sender;
- The identity of the recipient's financial institution;
- Any of the following items received with the transmittal order:
  - The name and address of the recipient
  - The account number of the recipient
  - Any other specific identifier of the recipient; and
- Any form relating to the transmittal of funds that is completed or signed by the person placing the order.

Note: Many MSBs do not maintain established customer relationships; therefore, they would be subject to recordkeeping requirements for other than established customers, in addition to the recordkeeping requirements outlined above.

If the sender is not an established customer, the MSB must verify the identity of the sender (unless the transmittal order is not made in person) and the following records also must be retained:[36]

- The sender's name and address;
- The type and number of identification reviewed (e.g., driver's license);
- The sender's taxpayer identification number (e.g., social security number, or, if none, alien identification number, passport number, and country of issuance, or notation in the record of the lack thereof). (If the MSB knows that the person

---

33. 31 CFR 103.33(b) and (c).
34. 31 CFR 103.33(f).
35. 31 CFR 103.33(f).
36. 31 CFR 103.33(f)(2).

placing the transmittal order is not the sender, the taxpayer identification number of the sender (e.g., social security number, or if none, alien identification number, passport number and country of issuance, or notation in the record of the lack thereof); and

- For transmittals not made in person, a copy or record of the method of payment (e.g., check or credit card transaction) in addition to the records listed above.

MSBs must maintain an original, microfilm, other copy, or electronic record of the transmittal order when it is acting as the receiving MSB for a recipient that is an established customer. If the recipient is not an established customer, the MSB must verify the identity of the person receiving the proceeds (unless the transmittal order is not made in person) and the following records must be retained:

- The original, microfilm, other copy, or electronic record of the transmittal order;
- The name and address;
- The type and number of the identification reviewed (e.g., driver's license);
- The recipient's taxpayer identification number (e.g., social security number, alien identification number, passport number and country of issuance);
- If the MSB knows that the person receiving the proceeds is not the recipient, the recipient's name, address, and taxpayer identification number (e.g., social security number, or if none, alien identification number, passport number and country of issuance, or notation in the record of the lack thereof); and
- If the proceeds are delivered other than in person, a copy of the check or other instrument to pay the transmittal, or the information contained on the check or other instrument, as well as the name and address of the person to whom it was sent.

Records to be Maintained by Currency Dealers or Exchangers

Currency dealers or exchangers are required to make and retain additional records.[37]

- A currency dealer or exchanger is required to secure and maintain a record of the taxpayer identification number of each person who opens a transaction account or is extended a line of credit within 30 days after an account is opened or credit line extended.

  - If the person is a non-resident alien, a record of the person's passport number or description of some other government document used to verify identity is required.

---

37. 31 CFR 103.37.

- ▪ If the account or credit line is in the names of two or more persons, a currency dealer or exchanger is required to secure the taxpayer identification number of a person having a financial interest in the account or credit line.[38]

If a currency dealer or exchanger is unable to secure a person's identification within the 30-day period, it will not be in violation if:

- A reasonable effort was made to secure the identification; and

- A list is maintained containing the names, addresses, and account or credit line numbers of those persons whose required identification could not be secured.[39]

The 30-day period may be extended if the person opening an account or credit line has applied for a taxpayer identification or social security number.[40] In addition, currency dealers or exchangers are required to retain either the original, microfilm, or other copy of the following records, to the extent that the business of the currency dealer or exchanger generates such records:[41]

- Statements of bank accounts, including paid checks, deposit slips, charges, or other debit or credit memoranda;

- Daily work records, including purchase and sales slips or other memoranda needed to identify and reconstruct currency transactions with customers and foreign banks;

- A record of each exchange of currency involving transactions in excess of $1,000 including the customer's name and address, passport number or taxpayer identification number, date and amount of the transaction, and currency name, country, and total amount of each foreign currency;

- Signature cards or other documents evidencing signature authority over each deposit or security account, containing the name, address, taxpayer identification number (TIN) or employer identification number (EIN) of the depositor, the signature of the depositor or other person authorized to sign on the account (if customer accounts are maintained in a code name, a record of the actual owner of the account);

- Each item, including checks, drafts, or transfers of credit, of more than $10,000 remitted or transferred to a person, account or place outside the United States;

- A record of each receipt of currency, other monetary instruments, investment securities, and checks, and of each transfer of funds or credit, or more than $10,000 received on any one occasion directly and not through a domestic financial institution from any person, account or place outside the United States;

---

38. 31 CFR 103.37(a)(1).

39. Id.

40. 31 CFR 103.37(a)(2).

41. 31 CFR 103.37(b).

- Records prepared or received by a dealer in the ordinary course of business, which would be needed to reconstruct an account and trace a check in excess of $100 deposited in such account through its internal recordkeeping system to its depository institution, or to supply a description of a deposited check in excess of $100;

- A record of the name, address, and TIN, if available, of any person presenting a certificate of deposit for payment, a description of the instrument, and date of the transaction; and

- A system of books and records that will enable the currency dealer or exchanger to prepare an accurate balance sheet and income statement.

Specific records that must be kept by MSBs are shown in the table at Appendix I – Chart of Recordkeeping Requirements.

Examination Procedures
Recordkeeping Requirements

Any documents the MSB maintains that are relevant to the BSA examination can be requested and reviewed. The examiner will determine if the MSB is maintaining adequate records and must document any recordkeeping violations. Procedures should be performed based on the risks identified by the examiner.

Records to be Maintained for Issuance or Sale of Money Orders/Traveler's Checks

1. Review the MSB's policies, procedures, and internal controls for collecting and maintaining required records for issuance and sale of money orders/traveler's checks. Determine if policies, procedures, and internal controls are appropriate to ensure compliance with recordkeeping requirements.

2. Review the MSB's records to determine if all the required information on the purchasers of money orders/traveler's checks involving currency in amounts of $3,000 to $10,000, inclusive, has been maintained and verified pursuant to the recordkeeping requirements.[42] Records should include:

   - Name and address of the purchaser. The MSB is required to verify the purchaser's name and address and record the specific identifying information (e.g., state of issuance and purchaser's driver's license number). When the purchaser is not an account holder, the MSB shall verify the purchaser's name and address by examination of a document that is normally acceptable within the banking community as a means of identification when cashing checks and that contains the name and address of the purchaser, and shall record the specific identifying information (e.g., state of issuance and purchaser's driver's license number);[43]

   - Date of purchase;

   - Type of instruments purchased;

   - Serial numbers of the instruments purchased;

   - Amount in dollars of each instrument purchased;

   - When the purchaser is not an account holder, the purchaser's social security number or alien identification number; and

   - When the purchaser is not an account holder, the purchaser's date of birth.

---

42. 31 CFR 103.29.

43. 31 CFR 103.29(a)(2)(ii).

3. Review the MSB's sales records and/or daily summaries for block purchases. Trace a sample of these purchases to records of sales of $3,000 to $10,000 in currency to determine if appropriate records are maintained. Verify that records are complete and procedures followed are consistent with the BSA/AML compliance policies, procedures, and internal controls established in the AML program.

Additional Procedures for Issuance or Sale of Money Orders/Traveler's Checks Based on Risk

4. Perform a sort of the MSB's transaction database for each type of instrument (money orders, traveler's checks, etc.,) for the period of time selected. The database should contain the following fields at minimum: date instrument was sold, time instrument was sold, instrument number, office (location) where instrument was sold, amount of instrument, fee or commission amount. For traveler's check issuers, request that the database contain a field indicating the beginning and ending numbers of the traveler's checks sold to each customer, as well as a field showing the total amount of the sale to each customer.

- For traveler's checks, sort the transactions by amount to determine sales totaling $3,000 to $10,000 in currency. Compare the results of the sort to the entries in the records provided by management and determine whether all the traveler's check sales totaling $3,000 to $10,000 in currency to one person contained in the sort are also included in the records provided by the MSB. Investigate any differences.

- For all other instruments, sort the transactions by instrument number and note any sequential sales of instruments within a short period of time sold at the same location totaling $3,000 to $10,000 in currency. For example, if it is noted that three individual sales of money orders occurred within seconds apart at the same location and the three transactions total in excess of $3,000, request the MSB to research the items and provide the purchaser information for the transactions.

- Compare the sequential transaction sets noted through the database sort to the transaction records provided by the MSB and determine whether all the sales totaling $3,000 to $10,000 in currency to one person contained in the sort are also included in the records provided by the MSB. Investigate any differences.

- Perform a sort of single transactions for the sample period where a customer conducts a transaction and the amount of the transaction is $3,000 to $10,000 in currency. Verify additional information is maintained. Fees are not included in the dollar thresholds. Are there obvious incorrect SSNs?

- Perform a sort for multiple transactions for the sample period - transactions where the customer conducts multiple transactions at the same location or different locations and the transaction amounts are $3,000 or more. The regulation requires aggregating the money order/traveler's check purchases if it can be shown that an employee, officer, or partner of the MSB has knowledge that the transactions have occurred. Prior to citing a possible violation, the examiner must show how the "knowledge" can be demonstrated. If it can be shown that a customer is conducting multiple transactions below the recordkeeping requirements, it may be an indication of possible suspicious activity and should be analyzed.

- Document and discuss any deficiencies identified.

5. Trace large block sales or large single-transaction sales of money orders/traveler's checks in the register or other similar reports to the records required for recordkeeping compliance purposes. A block sale involves the simultaneous sale of sequentially numbered money orders/traveler's checks for an amount at or near the maximum dollar amount. The issuing company usually sets the maximum amount allowed for each money order/traveler's check. The review should identify blocks of money orders/traveler's checks totaling $3,000 to $10,000 for recordkeeping requirements.

6. Determine the completeness of the money order/traveler's checks register by reconciling this to the summary sales reports sent to the issuing company, the discrepancy report from the issuing company, and the bank deposit records.

Records to be Maintained for Transmittals of Funds

7. Review the MSB's policies, procedures, and internal controls for collecting and maintaining required records for transmittals of funds. Determine if policies, procedures, and internal controls are appropriate to ensure compliance with recordkeeping requirements.

8. Review transmittal reports listing transactions of $3,000 or more for completeness and any obvious invalid data (e.g., false social security number (SSN)). These records may be maintained by the principal MSB, and when possible, the examiner should request an electronic file of the records relating to transactions of $3,000 or more.

9. Determine the adequacy of the MSB's customer identification policies by selecting a sample of transactions and verifying customer identification was obtained and verified as appropriate.

Additional Procedures for Transmittals of Funds Based on Risk

10. If the risk assessment, discussions with management, or review of policies and procedures suggest that transactions of $3,000 or more occurred, and that required records of these transactions might not have been maintained, sort the funds transmittals in the database provided by the MSB by transaction amount and determine whether all the transmittals of $3,000 or more contained all required information. Investigate any differences.

Records to be Maintained by Currency Dealers or Exchangers

11. Review the MSB's policies, procedures, and internal controls for collecting and maintaining required records for currency dealing or exchanging. Determine if policies, procedures, and internal controls are appropriate to ensure compliance with recordkeeping requirements.

12. Review a sample of transactions to determine whether required records have been maintained.[44]

Additional Procedures for Currency Dealers or Exchangers Based on Risk

13. Trace transactions to the transaction vouchers, checking for compliance with recordkeeping requirements.

Evaluating the MSB's Compliance with Recordkeeping Requirements

14. If a determination is made that records are inadequate or were destroyed or not maintained, the examiner should:

    • Expand the scope of the BSA examination; and

    • Document all problem areas and findings in the workpapers.

15. If apparent BSA violations are detected, the examiner should interview the responsible person or employee who conducted the unrecorded transaction(s). Based on the responses, the examiner should consider expanding the scope of the examination.

16. On the basis of examination procedures completed, including transaction testing, form a conclusion about the ability of policies, procedures, and processes to meet regulatory requirements associated with monitoring, collecting, and retaining information for recordkeeping.

---

44. 31 CFR 103.37.

Record Retention Requirements — Overview

Objective: *Assess the MSB's compliance with the respective statutory and regulatory record retention requirements as they apply to the MSB's financial services.*

31 CFR 103.38(d) is the overall authority for record retention. Generally, records must be retained for a period of five years from the date of the transaction. This five-year period is reaffirmed in 31 CFR 103.32 and 31 CFR 103.29 for foreign financial account records maintained by persons and for issuers and sellers of money orders, traveler's checks, etc. The terms of retention for records required to be maintained under a targeting order are contained in the targeting order. The five-year record retention for SAR-MSBs and supporting documentation is found in the regulations that establish a SAR-MSB requirement.

Failure to retain records is considered to be a recordkeeping violation.

Copies of all filed CTRs must be retained by the MSB for five years from the date of the report.[45]

Copies of all filed SAR-MSBs and the original or record of any supporting documentation shall be maintained for five years from the date of filing the SAR-MSB.[46]

All records created for the AML program requirements must be retained for five years.

A copy of the MSB registration (if applicable) must be retained for five years.

Current annual agent list and agent list(s) for the past five years must be maintained, if applicable.[47]

Copies of records required for transmittals of funds must be retained for five years.[48]

Copies of records required to be maintained for currency dealers or exchangers shall be retained for five years.[49]

---

45. 31 CFR 103.27(a)(3).
46. 31 CFR 103.20(c).
47. 31 CFR 103.41(d).
48. 31 CFR 103.38(d).
49. *Id.*

All records related to filed Reports of Foreign Bank and Financial Accounts (FBAR) (TD F 90-22.1) must be retained for five years.[50]

Check cashers are not required to maintain any additional records under BSA regulations. However, they are required to maintain records if they provide other money services in addition to check cashing.

In some circumstances, the principal MSB may retain records for its agent MSBs.

---

50. 31 CFR 103.32.

Examination Procedures
Record Retention Requirements

1. Through review of policies, procedures, internal controls, and transactional testing, ensure that:

   - Filed CTRs have been retained by the MSB for the required five-year period;

   - Filed SAR-MSBs have been retained by the MSB for the required five-year period;

   - All records related to filed FBARs have been retained by the MSB for the required five-year period;[51]

   - Records required to be maintained for the issuance and sale of money orders/traveler's checks have been retained by the MSB for the required five-year period;

   - Records required to be maintained for funds transmittals have been retained by the MSB for the required five-year period; and

   - Records required to be maintained for MSB registration (if applicable) have been retained by the MSB for five years.

2. Review the AML program, policies, procedures, and internal controls to determine if there is any record of the MSB maintaining the above mentioned documents and related information for five years. Make a reference in the procedure comment to the specific section or page number of the policy, procedure, or other document that references the five-year maintenance requirement. Also, confirm with management that the records are in fact maintained for five years, and document management's comments regarding this issue.

Evaluating the MSB's Compliance with Record Retention Requirements

3. If a determination is made that records are inadequate or have been destroyed or not maintained, the examiner should:

   - Expand the scope of the BSA examination; and

   - Document all problem areas and findings in the workpapers.

4. If apparent BSA violations are detected, the examiner should interview the responsible person or employee who conducted the undocumented transaction(s). Based on the responses, the examiner should consider expanding the scope of the examination.

5. On the basis of examination procedures completed, including transaction testing, form a conclusion about the ability of policies, procedures, and processes to meet regulatory requirements associated with record retention.

---

51. 31 CFR 103.32.

Currency Transaction Reporting — Overview

Objective: *Assess the MSB's compliance with statutory and regulatory requirements for the reporting of large currency transactions.*

An MSB must file a Currency Transaction Report (CTR) (FinCEN Form 104) for each transaction in currency[52] (deposit, withdrawal, exchange, or other payment or transfer) of more than $10,000 by, through, or to the MSB. A transaction that is a transfer of funds by means of bank check, funds transmittal, or other written order, and that does not include the physical transfer of currency, is not a transaction in currency for this purpose.

A CTR must be filed for all single currency transactions of more than $10,000 in one business day.[53] Multiple currency transactions must be aggregated, and a CTR is required if the business has knowledge that the multiple transactions are by or on behalf of any person and result in either currency in or out totaling more than $10,000 in one business day. The CTR must be filed within 15 calendar days (25 days if filed electronically or on magnetic media[54]) following the day the reportable transaction occurs.[55]

The evaluation of the MSB's ability to comply with its BSA reporting obligations is an important task within the BSA examination. The examiner will need to determine whether the MSB has filed required BSA report(s) timely and correctly.

The examiner should become familiar with the components of the summary records maintained by the MSB, including both the daily cash reconciliation and teller reconciliations.

Aggregation of Currency Transactions

Multiple currency transactions totaling more than $10,000 during any one business day are treated as a single transaction if the MSB has knowledge that they are by or on behalf of the same person. Transactions throughout the MSB should be aggregated when determining if multiple transactions should be treated as a single transaction.

---

52. Currency is defined as coin and paper money of the United States or any other country as long as it (1) is designated as legal tender, (2) routinely circulates, and (3) is customarily accepted as money in the country of issue.

53. 31 CFR 103.22(b)(1).

54. From January 1, 2009, MSBs, like other financial institutions, will no longer be able to file on magnetic media.

55. 31 CFR 103.27(a)(1).

MSBs are strongly encouraged to develop systems necessary to aggregate currency transactions throughout the MSB. Management should ensure that an adequate system is implemented that will appropriately report currency transactions subject to the BSA requirement.

Filing Time Frames and Record Retention Requirements

A completed CTR must be filed with FinCEN within 15 days after the date of the transaction (25 days if filed electronically or on magnetic media[56]). The MSB must retain copies of CTRs for five years from the date of the report.[57]

CTR Back Filing

If an MSB discovers that it has failed to file CTRs on reportable transactions, the MSB should begin filing CTRs and should contact the Internal Revenue Service (IRS) ECC-D[58] to request a determination on whether it is necessary to back file transactions that should have been reported.

---

56. Effective January 1, 2009, MSBs, like other financial institutions, will no longer be able to file on magnetic media.

57. 31 CFR 103.27(a)(3).

58. The IRS ECC-D is the central repository for the BSA reports that financial institutions must file. The IRS ECC-D can be contacted at 800-800-2877.

Examination Procedures
Currency Transaction Reporting

1. Determine whether the MSB's policies, procedures, and processes adequately address the preparation, filing, and retention of Currency Transaction Reports (CTRs) (FinCEN Form 104).

2. Review correspondence that the MSB has received from the IRS ECC-D relating to incorrect or incomplete CTRs (errors). Determine whether management has taken corrective action, when necessary.

3. Review the currency transaction system. This review includes determining whether the MSB has met its requirements for filing CTRs for all currency transactions where the MSB either receives or pays out currency in excess of $10,000. Determine whether the MSB aggregates all or some currency transactions. Determine whether the MSB aggregates transactions by taxpayer identification number (TIN), individual taxpayer identification number (ITIN), employer identification number (EIN), or customer information file (CIF) number. Does the MSB ensure that multiple currency transactions are treated as a single transaction if they result in either currency in or out totaling more than $10,000 during any one business day to the same person? Also, evaluate how CTRs are filed on customers with missing TINs or EINs.

4. Determine if the MSB's independent testing confirms the integrity and accuracy of the management information systems (MIS) used for aggregating currency transactions. If this was not done, the examiner should confirm the integrity and accuracy of the MIS. The examiner's review should confirm that tellers do not have the capability to override currency aggregation systems.

Transaction Testing

Transactional testing should be used to support the examiner's preliminary conclusions on the adequacy of the MSB's AML program.

5. On the basis of a risk assessment, prior examination reports, and a review of the MSB's independent review findings, select a sample of filed CTRs (hard copy or from computer-generated filings) to determine whether:

   - CTRs are completed in accordance with FinCEN instructions;

   - CTRs are filed accurately and completely. The Web CBRS database should also be checked to verify that the reports were actually filed;

- CTRs were filed within 15 days (25 days if filed electronically or on magnetic media[59]) from the date the transaction(s) occurred. Compare and cross-reference the date(s) of the reportable transaction(s) to the transaction date(s) shown on the CTR. Count the number of days between the date of the CTR and the transaction date(s) to ensure the number of days is not in excess of 15 (25 days if filed electronically or on magnetic media). If the Web CBRS database was queried, compare the dates for the CTRs shown by the query to the filing date on the CTR forms provided by the MSB. Note any differences in dates. If there are significant differences between the dates shown by the query and the dates shown on the CTRs provided by management, discuss with management; and

- Check for discrepancies between the MSB's records of CTRs and the CTRs reflected in the download from the Web CBRS. The MSB retains copies of CTRs for five years from the date of the report.[60]

6. The examiner may perform additional transaction testing to include a risk-based sample of transaction records to determine CTRs were filed where appropriate.

   - Review transaction records, system-generated reports, money transmission logs, etc., and review transactions where a customer conducted a transaction and the amount of the transaction plus the fee charged aggregated greater than $10,000 in currency.

   - Review transaction records, system-generated reports, money transmission logs, etc., and review transactions where the customer conducted multiple transactions at the same location or different locations and the transaction amounts plus the fees aggregated greater than $10,000 in currency. Note: For money transmission records, this should be completed for both customers sending funds and recipients of funds at a branch or agent located in the United States.

   - If the examiner determines a CTR should have been filed or the required recordkeeping or reporting requirements are not met, the examiner should determine the reason the internal procedures failed.

7. If apparent BSA violations are detected, the examiner should interview the responsible person or employee who conducted the transaction. Based on the responses, the examiner should consider expanding the scope of the examination. When the MSB contends that a CTR was filed and provides its retained copy as evidence, the examiner should query the Web CBRS database and conduct an exhaustive search before concluding that a CTR was not received. In conducting the search, the examiner should query all customer numerical identification fields on the CTR such as account number (if applicable), SSN, and identification credential number.

---

59. Effective January 1, 2009, MSBs, like other financial institutions, will no longer be able to file on magnetic media.

60. 31 CFR 103.27(a)(3).

Additional Examination Procedures for Check Cashers Based on Risk

8. Based on the risk posed by the MSB, the examiner may consider the following steps when reviewing check casher's records:

   - Review copies of cashed checks or other available records for transactions over $10,000 requiring CTR filing and determine if CTRs were filed. This includes multiple transactions for the same payee where the total currency exceeds $10,000 in one business day.

   - Trace a sample of teller reconciliation summary totals to the daily cash reconciliation to determine if CTRs were filed when required.

   - Trace a sample of daily cash reconciliation totals to the daily bank deposit slips to determine if CTRs were filed when required.

   - Trace a sample of the daily cash reconciliations to the bank statements to determine whether all CTRs were filed when required.

   - Analyze the bank reconciliations, cash-on-hand records, and transaction records to identify large transactions. The examiner should look for decreases in either the amount of ending cash on hand or amounts withdrawn from the MSB's bank. Large decreases or withdrawals of cash could indicate large checks were cashed. The examiner should note the dates when amounts could exceed $10,000 or transactions appear to be structured to avoid the $10,000 threshold.

   - Analyze the transaction records for cash in and cash out transactions conducted by the MSB to determine if CTRs are filed when appropriate.

   - Perform a review of records to determine if CTRs are filed for large currency transactions, identified by tellers' cash proof sheets, automated large currency transaction systems, or other types of aggregation systems that cover all relevant areas of the MSB.

Additional Examination Procedures for Issuance or Sale of Money Orders/Traveler's Checks Based on Risk

9. Trace large block sales or large single-transaction sales of money orders/traveler's checks in the money order/traveler's check register or other similar records to the records required for CTR reporting. A block sale involves the simultaneous sale of sequentially numbered money orders/traveler's checks for an amount at or near the maximum dollar amount. The issuing company usually sets the maximum amount allowed for each money order/traveler's check. The review should identify blocks of money orders/traveler's checks greater than $10,000 for CTR reporting.

10. Analyze the summary and transaction records for cash in and cash out for transactions conducted by the MSB.

Additional Examination Procedures for Money Transmitters Based on Risk

11. Perform a sort of transmission records. Analyze customer database sorts to detect unreported transactions, errors, and/or deficiencies in the money transmitter's BSA compliance system for reporting CTRs. (The examiner should review such information as the name, address, dollar amounts of transmissions, social security number, and phone number.)

    • Compare the results of the transaction database sort for transactions greater than $10,000 to the CTR forms provided by the MSB. For example, if the sort indicates the MSB conducted 25 transactions of more than $10,000 for the period, you should typically see at least 25 CTRs filed for the period. However, some transactions of more than $10,000 may not involve currency aggregating more than $10,000, and would not require the filing of a CTR. For example, a customer may pay for an $11,000 money transmission with $6,000 in cash and $5,000 in another form of payment. For transactions of more than $10,000 that do not involve currency of more than $10,000, request that the MSB provide documentation (copies of checks, breakdown of currency and negotiable instruments, etc.) to support the reason for not filing a CTR.

    • Use the results of the transaction database sort for transactions conducted by the same person on the same business day to determine if CTRs were filed for the transaction aggregations showing in the database sort. Note aggregations showing customers who conduct transactions at multiple branch or agent locations of the MSB.

    • If CTRs for the aggregations noted in the database sort cannot be found, discuss with management and determine why CTRs were not filed for the aggregations noted. One likely reason could be that currency totaling more than $10,000 was not involved in the transactions. Request documentation from management to support why CTRs were not filed for the aggregated amounts totaling more than $10,000 by one person in one business day.

12. Analyze the summary and transaction records for cash in and cash out for transactions conducted by the MSB.

Additional Examination Procedures for Currency Dealers or Exchangers Based on Risk

13. Select dates within the examination period and reconcile the transaction vouchers, daily transaction log, client ledger, and monthly and annual summary sheets.

14. Analyze the summary and transaction records for cash in and cash out for transactions conducted by the MSB. All large or unusual items should be pursued to ensure adequacy of CTR reporting.

15. Analyze database sorts of the name, address, and phone number fields to determine whether there were unreported transactions and deficiencies in the MSB's AML program.

Evaluating the MSB's Compliance with Currency Transaction Reporting Requirements

16. If a determination is made that records are inadequate or have been destroyed or not maintained, the examiner should:

    - Expand the scope of the BSA examination; and

    - Document all problem areas and findings in the workpapers.

17. If apparent BSA violations are detected, the examiner should interview the responsible person or employee who conducted the transaction. Based on the responses, the examiner should consider expanding the scope of the examination.

18. On the basis of examination procedures completed, including transaction testing, form a conclusion about the ability of policies, procedures, and processes to meet regulatory requirements associated with monitoring, detecting, and reporting for currency transactions.

Suspicious Activity Reporting – Overview

Objective: *Assess the MSB's policies, procedures, and processes, and its overall compliance with statutory and regulatory requirements for monitoring, detecting, and reporting suspicious activities.*

Suspicious activity reporting forms the cornerstone of the BSA reporting system. They provide financial information that is critical to the United States' ability to combat terrorist financing, money laundering, and other financial crimes. Examiners should focus on evaluating an MSB's overall policies, procedures, and processes to identify and research suspicious activity. However, as part of the examination process, examiners should also review individual SAR-MSB filing decisions to determine the effectiveness of the suspicious activity monitoring and reporting process. Above all, examiners and MSBs should recognize that the quality of SAR-MSB data is paramount to the effective implementation of the suspicious activity reporting system.

MSBs have different requirements for filing Suspicious Activity Reports, depending on the type of financial service provided to the public. For example, an MSB acting **solely as a check cashing business is exempt from SAR-MSB requirements.** Accordingly, examiners must be aware of the suspicious activity reporting requirements that apply to the particular MSB they are examining.

MSBs that provide money transmission or currency dealing or exchange – or businesses that issue, sell, or redeem money orders/traveler's checks – must report suspicious activity involving any transaction or pattern of transactions at or above **$2,000. However, see "Clearance Review--$5,000 threshold" for the threshold that applies to issuers of money orders/traveler's checks in certain situations. MSBs may voluntarily file SAR-MSBs for amounts below the required reporting thresholds.**

A Suspicious Activity Report must be filed if a transaction is conducted or attempted by, at, or through an MSB, *and* it involves or aggregates funds or other assets of at least $2,000, *and* the MSB knows, suspects, or has reason to suspect that the transaction (or pattern of transactions):

- Involves funds derived from illegal activity, or is intended to hide or disguise funds or assets derived from illegal activity, as part of a plan to violate or evade any federal law or regulation, or to avoid any transaction reporting requirement under federal law or regulation;

- Is designed, whether by structuring or other means, to evade any requirements of the BSA;

- Serves no business or apparent lawful purpose, and the reporting MSB knows of no reasonable explanation for the transaction after examining the available facts, including the background and possible purpose of the transaction; or

- Involves the use of the MSB to facilitate criminal activity.

Factors that should contribute to the decision to file a SAR-MSB include the following:

- The size, frequency, and nature of the transaction;

- The MSB's experience with the customer and other individuals or entities associated with the transaction (if any); and

- The norm for such transactions within the MSB's line of business and geographic area.

It is important to note that a large transaction is not necessarily suspicious.

Clearance Review - $5,000 Threshold

For issuers of money orders/traveler's checks, to the extent that the identification of suspicious transactions is derived from a review of clearance records or other similar records of money orders/traveler's checks that have been sold or processed, the issuer is required to report a suspicious transaction or pattern of transactions that involves or aggregates funds or other assets of at least $5,000. MSBs may voluntarily file SAR-MSBs for suspicious transactions that are below the required reporting threshold.

Systems to Identify, Research, and Report Suspicious Activity

Policies, procedures, and internal controls should identify the person(s) responsible for the identification, research, and reporting of suspicious activities. Appropriate policies, procedures, and processes should be in place to monitor and identify unusual activity. The level of monitoring should be dictated by the MSB's assessment of risk, with particular emphasis on high-risk products, services, customers, geographic locations, etc. Monitoring systems typically include some combination of employee identification, manual systems, and automated systems. The MSB should ensure adequate staff is assigned to the identification, research, and reporting of suspicious activities, taking into account the MSB's overall risk profile and the volume of transactions. After thorough research and analysis, decisions to file or not to file a SAR-MSB should be documented. Note: There is no affirmative requirement to document decisions not to file SAR-MSBs, so an MSB should not be automatically criticized or cited for failing to have such documents. The lack of documentation may however make it more difficult to determine why the MSB decided not to file a SAR-MSB at the time it made the decision. The monitoring process may involve review of daily reports, reports that cover a period of time (e.g., rolling 30-day reports, monthly reports), or both types of reports. The type and frequency of reviews and resulting reports should be commensurate with the MSB's BSA/AML risk profile and should appropriately cover its high-risk products, services, customers, geographic locations, etc.

Manual Transaction Monitoring

A manual transaction monitoring system involves manual review of various reports generated by the MSB's management information systems (MIS) or vendor systems. Some MSBs' MIS are supplemented by vendor systems designed to identify reportable currency transactions and to maintain required funds transfer records. Many of these vendor systems include filtering models for the identification of unusual activity. Examples of MIS reports include currency activity reports, funds transfer reports, and monetary instrument sales reports. MIS or vendor system-generated reports typically allow the user to select a discretionary dollar threshold. Thresholds selected by management for the production of transaction reports should be appropriate for management to detect unusual activity. Upon identification of unusual activity, assigned personnel should review reasonably available information to determine whether the activity is suspicious. Management should periodically evaluate the appropriateness of filtering criteria and thresholds used in the monitoring process.

Transmittals of Funds Records

The BSA requires MSBs to maintain records of funds transmittals in amounts of $3,000 and above. Periodic review of this information can assist MSBs in identifying patterns of unusual activity. MSBs must report transactions or patterns of transactions at or above $2,000 that are suspicious. For MSBs with significant funds transmittal activity, use of spreadsheet or vendor software is an efficient way to review activity for unusual patterns. Many vendor software systems include standard suspicious activity filter reports. These reports typically focus on identifying transactions involving certain high-risk geographic locations and large funds transmittals. Each MSB should establish its own filtering criteria for both individuals and businesses.

Money Orders/Traveler's Checks Records

The BSA requires MSBs to maintain records of money order/traveler's check sales in the amount of $3,000 to $10,000 in currency. Periodic review of these records can assist MSBs in identifying patterns of unusual activity, such as currency structuring through the purchase of money orders/traveler's checks. MSBs must report transactions or patterns of transactions at or above $2,000 that are suspicious. To the extent that the identification of suspicious transactions is derived from a review of clearance records or other similar records of money orders/traveler's checks that have been sold or processed, the issuer is required to report a transaction or pattern of transactions that involves or aggregates funds or other assets of at least $5,000. MSBs should establish risk-based procedures to review these records periodically for unusual activity. An MSB may review these records to identify frequent purchasers or payees of money orders/ traveler's checks.

Currency Dealers or Exchangers Records

The BSA requires MSBs to maintain records of currency dealing or exchanges of more than $1,000. Periodic review of these records can assist MSBs in identifying patterns of unusual activity, such as currency structuring through currency exchanges done by the same individual. MSBs must report transactions or patterns of transactions at or above $2,000 that are suspicious. MSBs should establish risk-based procedures to periodically review these records for unusual activity.

Automated Monitoring

Automated monitoring systems typically use computer programs, developed in-house or purchased from vendors, to identify individual transactions, patterns of unusual activity, or deviations from expected activity. These systems can capture a wide range of account activity, such as money order/traveler's check sales and in-clearings and funds transmittals directly from the MSB's core data processing system. Large MSBs that operate in many locations or have a large volume of high-risk customers typically use automated account-monitoring systems.

Current types of automated systems include rule-based and intelligent systems. Rule-based systems detect unusual transactions that are outside of system-developed or management-established "rules." Such systems can consist of few or many rules, depending on the complexity of the in-house or vendor product. These rules are applied using a series of transaction filters or a rules engine. Rule-based automated systems are more sophisticated than the basic manual system, which only filters on one rule (e.g., transaction greater than $10,000). Rule-based automated monitoring systems can apply complex or multiple filters.

Intelligent systems are adaptive systems that can change their analysis over time on the basis of activity patterns, recent trends, changes in the customer base, and other relevant data. Intelligent systems review transactions in the context of customer profiles and other transactions.

Understanding the filtering criteria of a software-based monitoring system is critical to assessing the effectiveness of an automated monitoring system. System filtering criteria should be developed through a review of specific high-risk customers, products, and services. System filtering criteria, including specific profiles and rules, should be based on what is reasonable and expected for each type of customer. Monitoring customers purely on the basis of historical activity can be misleading if an individual customer's activity is not actually consistent with the activity of that customer's "type." If a customer's historical transaction activity is substantially different from what would normally be expected from that type of customer, continuing consistency with the customer's own historical activity does not address the question of whether the customer's pattern of activity is suspicious given its divergence from patterns of activity typical for other similar customers.

The authority to establish or change expected activity profiles should be clearly defined and should generally require the approval of the BSA compliance officer or senior management. Controls should ensure limited access to the monitoring system. Management should document or be able to explain filtering criteria, thresholds used, and how both are appropriate for the MSB's risks. Management should also periodically review the filtering criteria and thresholds to ensure that they are still appropriate and effective. In addition, the monitoring system's programming methodology and effectiveness should be independently validated to ensure that the models are detecting potentially suspicious activity.

Identifying Underlying Crime

MSBs are required to report suspicious activities above prescribed dollar thresholds that may involve money laundering, BSA violations, terrorist financing,[61] and certain other crimes. However, MSBs cannot be expected and are not required to investigate or confirm the underlying crime (e.g., terrorist financing, money laundering, tax evasion, identity theft, or fraud). Investigation is the responsibility of law enforcement. When evaluating suspicious activity and completing the SAR-MSB, MSBs should, to the best of their ability, identify the characteristics of the suspicious activity.

Law Enforcement Inquiries and Requests

MSBs should establish policies, procedures, and processes for identifying subjects of law enforcement requests, monitoring the transaction activity of those subjects, identifying unusual or suspicious activity related to those subjects, and filing SAR-MSBs related to those subjects, if warranted. Law enforcement inquiries and requests can include grand jury subpoenas or National Security Letters (NSLs).

---

61. If an MSB knows, suspects, or has reason to suspect that a customer may be linked to terrorist activity against the United States, it should immediately call FinCEN's Financial Institutions Hotline at the toll-free number: 866-556-3974. Similarly, if any other suspected violation — such as an ongoing money laundering scheme — requires immediate attention, the MSB should notify an appropriate law enforcement authority or agency. In either case, it must also file a SAR.

Mere receipt of a law enforcement inquiry does not, by itself, require the MSB to file a SAR-MSB. Nonetheless, a law enforcement inquiry may be relevant to an MSB's overall risk assessment of its customers. For example, the receipt of a grand jury subpoena should cause an MSB to review activity for the relevant customer.[62] It is incumbent upon an MSB to assess all of the information it knows about its customer, including the receipt of a law enforcement inquiry, in accordance with its risk-based AML program. The MSB should determine whether a SAR-MSB should be filed based on all customer information available, not on any one piece of information.

Additionally, because of the confidentiality of grand jury proceedings and their contents, an MSB should refrain from referencing in the SAR-MSB the fact that the MSB received a grand jury subpoena. Rather, the SAR-MSB should reference only those facts and activities that support the MSB's independent identification of unusual or suspicious transactions. Similarly, if the MSB receives any other law enforcement inquiry, the SAR-MSB should only reference the facts and activities supporting the MSB's identification of the transaction without referencing the law enforcement inquiry.

SAR-MSB Decision-Making Process

The MSB should have policies, procedures, and processes for referring unusual activity from all business lines to the personnel or department responsible for evaluating unusual activity, which may include senior management of the MSB. Upon identification of unusual activity, additional research is typically conducted. The MSB will generally have to make two decisions once it becomes aware of unusual activity related to a transaction:

- Whether to file a SAR-MSB; and
- Regardless of whether a SAR-MSB is filed, whether to monitor the customer going forward.

The MSB could decide, after review of all information, that the transaction does not warrant reporting. Notwithstanding that decision, the MSB could decide that it is appropriate to monitor the customer for the same or similar transactions in the future. The MSB could plan to revisit the question of whether to file a SAR-MSB if the customer conducts such transactions in the future. Alternatively, the MSB could have made the decision that it will file a SAR-MSB if such transactions continue without a reasonable explanation.

---

62. Bank Secrecy Act Advisory Group, "Section 5 — Issues and Guidance" *The SAR Activity Review – Trends, Tips & Issues*, Issue 10, May 2006, pages 42 – 44, at www.fincen.gov.

MSBs are encouraged to document SAR-MSB decisions. Thorough documentation provides a record of the SAR-MSB decision-making process, including final decisions not to file a SAR-MSB. However, due to the variety of systems used to identify, track, and report suspicious activity, as well as the fact that each suspicious activity reporting decision will be based on unique facts and circumstances, this documentation may not always look the same. It is the responsibility of the MSB to determine the sufficiency and adequacy of its documentation for the SAR-MSB decision-making process. There is no requirement that the process be in written format when the MSB determines not to file a SAR-MSB.[63] The lack of documentation may however make it more difficult to determine why the MSB decided not to file a SAR-MSB at the time it made the decision.

An MSB must file FinCEN Form 109 (the SAR-MSB, formerly Treasury Department Form TD 90-22.56) if the MSB knows, suspects, or has reason to suspect suspicious activities have occurred.[64]

- A SAR-MSB must be filed for suspicious transactions of at least $2,000 in funds or other assets conducted or attempted by, at, or through the MSB.[65]

- An MSB is required to file the SAR-MSB with FinCEN, through the ECC-D, no later than 30 calendar days after the date of detection.[66]

- MSBs are prohibited from notifying any person involved in the transaction that a SAR-MSB has been filed.[67]

Although check cashers are not required to file the SAR-MSB, they may elect to voluntarily file SAR-MSBs if they know, suspect, or have reason to suspect suspicious activities have occurred.[68] Check cashers are subject to the suspicious activity reporting rules to the extent that:

- Check cashers redeem either money orders/traveler's checks for currency or other monetary or negotiable instruments and hence qualify as redeemers of money orders/traveler's checks; or

- Check cashers also offer money transmission or money orders/traveler's checks, which are subject to suspicious activity reporting requirements.

---

63. Bank Secrecy Act Advisory Group, "Section 4 — Tips on SAR Form Preparation & Filing," *The SAR Activity Review* — Trends, Tips & Issues, Issue 10, May 2006, page 38, at www.fincen.gov.

64. 31 CFR 103.20(a).

65. 31 CFR 103.20(a)(2).

66. 31 CFR 103.20(b)(3).

67. 31 CFR 103.20(d).

68. 31 CFR 103.20.

Timing of a SAR-MSB Filing

A SAR must be filed no later than 30 calendar days from the date of the initial detection of facts that may constitute a basis for filing a SAR-MSB. MSBs may need to review a customer's transactions or account activity to determine whether to file a SAR-MSB. The need for a review of customer activity or transactions does not necessarily indicate a need to file a SAR-MSB. The time period for filing a SAR-MSB starts when the MSB, during its review or because of other factors, knows, suspects, or has reason to suspect that the activity or transactions under review meet one or more of the definitions of suspicious activity.[69]

The phrase "initial detection" should not be interpreted as meaning the moment a transaction is highlighted for review. There are a variety of legitimate transactions that could raise a red flag simply because they are inconsistent with a customer's normal activity. The MSB's automated monitoring system may flag the transaction; however, this should not be considered initial detection of potential suspicious activity.[70]

Whenever possible, an expeditious review of the transaction is recommended and can be of significant assistance to law enforcement. In any event, the review should be completed in a reasonable period of time. What constitutes a "reasonable period of time" will vary according to the facts and circumstances of the particular matter being reviewed and the effectiveness of the suspicious activity monitoring, reporting, and decision-making process of each MSB.

The key factors are that an MSB has established adequate procedures for reviewing and assessing facts and circumstances identified as potentially suspicious, that those procedures are documented, and that the MSB has followed those procedures.[71]

For violations requiring immediate attention, in addition to filing a timely SAR-MSB, an MSB is required to immediately notify, by telephone, an "appropriate law enforcement authority." For this notification, an "appropriate law enforcement authority" would generally be the local office of the Internal Revenue Service – Criminal Investigation Division or the FBI.

---

69. Bank Secrecy Act Advisory Group, "Section 5 — Issues and Guidance," *The SAR Activity Review – Trends, Tips & Issues*, Issue 1, October 2000, page 27, at www.fincen.gov.

70. Bank Secrecy Act Advisory Group, "Section 5 — Issues and Guidance," *The SAR Activity Review – Trends, Tips & Issues*, Issue 10, May 2006, page 44, at www.fincen.gov.

71. Id.

SAR-MSB Filing on Continuing Activity

One purpose of filing SAR-MSBs is to identify violations or potential violations of law to the appropriate law enforcement authorities for criminal investigation. This objective is accomplished by the filing of a SAR-MSB that identifies the activity of concern. If the apparently illegal activity continues over a period of time, such information should be made known directly to law enforcement, as well as to appropriate state and federal regulatory agencies. FinCEN's guidelines suggest that MSBs should report continuing suspicious activity by filing a report at least every 90 days.[72] This will notify law enforcement of the continuing nature of the activity, as well as remind the MSB that it should continue to review the suspicious activity to determine whether other actions may be appropriate, such as management determining that it is necessary to terminate the relationship with the customer or employee that gives rise to the filing.

SAR-MSB Quality

MSBs are required to file SAR-MSB forms that are complete, thorough, and timely. MSBs should include all known suspect information on the SAR-MSB form, and the importance of the accuracy of this information cannot be overstated. Inaccurate information on the SAR-MSB form, or an incomplete or disorganized narrative, may make further analysis difficult, if not impossible. However, there may be legitimate reasons why certain information may not be provided in a SAR-MSB, such as when the filer does not have the information.

A thorough and complete narrative may make the difference in whether law enforcement understands the described conduct and its possible criminal nature. Because the SAR-MSB narrative section is the only area summarizing suspicious activity, the narrative section, as stated on the SAR-MSB form, is "critical." Thus, a failure to adequately describe the factors making a transaction or activity suspicious undermines the purpose of the SAR-MSB.

By their nature, SAR-MSB narratives are subjective, and examiners generally should not criticize the MSB's interpretation of the facts. Nevertheless, MSBs should ensure that SAR-MSB narratives are complete, thoroughly describe the extent and nature of the suspicious activity, and are included within the SAR-MSB form (attachments to the narrative section are of no value, as they will not be available to users of FinCEN's database of BSA reports). More specific guidance is available in Appendix E – FinCEN SAR Quality Guidance and Appendix F – SAR Supporting Documentation Guidance to assist MSBs in writing SAR-MSB narratives, and assist examiners in evaluating them. In addition, comprehensive guidance is available from FinCEN ("Guidance on Preparing a Complete & Sufficient Suspicious Activity Report Narrative") at www.fincen.gov.

---

72. Bank Secrecy Act Advisory Group, "Section 5 — Issues and Guidance," *The SAR Activity Review*, Issue 1, October 2000, page 27 at www.fincen.gov.

Prohibition of SAR-MSB Disclosure

No MSB that reports a suspicious transaction, or any director, officer, employee or agent of the MSB, may notify any person involved in the transaction that the transaction has been reported. Additionally, no officer or employee of the Federal Government or of any state, local, tribal, or territorial government within the United States, who has any knowledge that such report was made, may disclose to any person involved in the transaction that the transaction has been reported, other than as necessary to fulfill the official duties of such officer or employee.[73] Any person subpoenaed or otherwise requested to disclose a SAR-MSB or the information contained in a SAR-MSB, except when such disclosure is requested by FinCEN or an appropriate law enforcement or supervisory agency,[74] shall decline to produce the SAR-MSB or to provide any information that would disclose that a SAR-MSB has been prepared or filed, citing 31 CFR 103.20(d) and 31 USC 5318(g)(2). FinCEN should be notified of any such request and of the MSB's response.

Safe Harbor

An MSB that files a SAR-MSB (whether required or voluntarily), and any director, officer, employee or agent of the MSB, shall be protected from liability for any disclosure contained in, or for failure to disclose the fact of, such report, or both, to the extent provided by 31 USC 5318(g)(3).

---

73. 31 USC 5318(g)(2).

74. Examples of agencies to which a SAR or the information contained therein could be provided include: the criminal investigative services of the armed forces; the Bureau of Alcohol, Tobacco, and Firearms; an attorney general, district attorney, or state's attorney at the state or local level; the Drug Enforcement Administration; the Federal Bureau of Investigation; the Internal Revenue Service or tax enforcement agencies at the state level; the Office of Foreign Assets Control; a state or local police department; a United States Attorney's Office; Immigration and Customs Enforcement; the U.S. Postal Inspection Service; and the U.S. Secret Service. For additional information, refer to *The SAR Activity Review*, Issue 9, October 2005, page 44 at www.fincen.gov.

Examination Procedures
Suspicious Activity Reporting

Review of Policies, Procedures, and Processes

1. Review the MSB's policies, procedures, and processes for identifying, researching, and reporting suspicious activity. Determine whether they include the following:

   - Lines of communication for the referral of unusual activity to appropriate personnel;

   - Designation of individual(s) responsible for identifying, researching, and reporting suspicious activities;

   - Monitoring systems used to identify unusual activity;

   - Procedures to ensure the timely generation of, review of, and response to reports used to identify unusual activities;

   - Procedures for documenting decisions not to file a SAR-MSB. (Note: There is no affirmative requirement to document decisions not to file SAR-MSBs, so an MSB should not be automatically criticized or cited for failing to have such documentation. The lack of documentation, however, may make it far more difficult to determine the decision process for not filing a SAR-MSB);

   - Procedures for determining whether to refuse services to customers for attempting a suspicious transaction or engaging in continuous suspicious activity;

   - Procedures for completing, filing, and retaining SAR-MSBs and their supporting documentation; and

   - Procedures for reporting SAR-MSBs to senior management.

Evaluating Suspicious Activity Monitoring Systems

Review the MSB's monitoring systems and how they fit into the MSB's overall suspicious activity monitoring and reporting process. Complete the appropriate examination procedures that follow. When evaluating the effectiveness of the MSB's monitoring systems, examiners should consider the MSB's overall risk profile.

Manual Transaction Monitoring

2. Review the MSB's transaction monitoring reports. Determine whether the reports capture all areas that pose money laundering and terrorist financing risks. Examples of these reports include: currency activity reports, funds transfer reports, monetary instrument sales reports, large item reports, and zero fee transaction reports.

3. Determine whether the MSB's monitoring systems use reasonable filtering criteria whose programming has been independently verified. Determine whether the monitoring systems generate accurate reports at a reasonable frequency.

Automated Transaction Monitoring

4. Identify the types of customers, products, and services that are included within the automated monitoring system.

5. Identify the system's methodology for establishing and applying expected activity or profile filtering criteria and for generating monitoring reports.

   - Determine whether the system's filtering criteria are reasonable.

   - Determine whether the programming of the methodology has been independently validated.

   - Determine that controls ensure limited access to the monitoring system and sufficient oversight of assumption changes.

Evaluating the SAR-MSB Decision-Making Process

6. Evaluate the MSB's policies, procedures, and processes for referring unusual activity from all business lines to the personnel or department responsible for evaluating unusual activity.

7. Determine whether policies, procedures, and processes require appropriate research when monitoring and reporting unusual activity. Note: The decision to file a SAR-MSB is an inherently subjective judgment. Examiners should focus on whether the MSB has an effective suspicious activity reporting decision-making process, not on decisions about whether to file individual SAR-MSBs. Examiners may review individual SAR-MSB filing decisions as a means to test the effectiveness of the suspicious activity monitoring, reporting, and decision-making process. In those instances where the MSB has an adequate, established suspicious activity reporting decision-making process, followed existing policies, procedures, and processes, and determined not to file a SAR-MSB, the MSB should not be criticized for the failure to file a SAR-MSB unless the failure is significant or accompanied by evidence of bad faith.

8. Review SAR-MSB activity. Have there been significant changes in the volume or nature of SAR-MSBs filed? Investigate the reason(s) for these change(s).

   - If there is a significant historical change in the number and/or nature of SAR-MSBs filed, interview responsible personnel to determine whether the changes are appropriate. Determine whether management is aware of trends identified.

   - Review the nature of SAR-MSBs filed.

   - Determine whether management has a process to monitor the number and nature of SAR-MSBs filed and the ability to strengthen controls and processes when necessary, based on this information.

Transaction Testing

Transactional testing is used to support the examiner's preliminary conclusions on the adequacy of the MSB's suspicious activity monitoring and reporting process.

SAR-MSB Reporting

9. On the basis of a risk assessment, prior examination reports, policies, procedures, internal controls, and the MSB's preliminary examination findings, sample the SAR-MSBs downloaded from the BSA reporting database or the MSB's internal SAR-MSB records. Review the quality of SAR-MSB data to assess the following:

   - SAR-MSBs contain accurate information;

   - SAR-MSB narratives are complete and thorough, and clearly explain why the activity is suspicious;

   - SAR-MSBs were filed within the required timeframe; and

   - SAR-MSBs were actually filed (verification of filing through the Web CBRS database).

Testing the Suspicious Activity Monitoring System

10. Sample specific customer transactions to review the following:

    - Suspicious activity monitoring reports; and

    - Decisions not to file a SAR-MSB. (Note: There is no affirmative requirement to document decisions not to file SAR-MSBs so an MSB should not be automatically criticized or cited for failing to have such documentation. The lack of documentation, however, may make it far more difficult to determine why the MSB decided not to file a SAR-MSB at the time it made the decision.)

    (Transaction testing of suspicious activity monitoring systems and reporting processes is intended to determine whether the MSB's policies, procedures, and processes are adequate and effectively implemented. Transaction testing of suspicious activity monitoring systems and reporting processes should be based on the risks identified during the examiner's review of the MSB's risk assessment as well as the policies, procedures, and internal controls implemented by the MSB to mitigate risks, identify suspicious activity, and report suspicious activity. Examiners should document the factors they used to select samples and should maintain a list of the SAR-MSBs or transactions sampled.)

11. For the transactions selected previously, obtain the following customer information, if applicable:

    - Selected sample of transaction activity covering the total customer relationship and showing all transactions;

    - Supporting documentation; and

    - Other relevant information and correspondence;

Review the selected transactions for unusual activity. If the examiner identifies unusual activity, review customer information for indications that the activity is typical for the customer (i.e., the sort of activity in which the customer is normally expected to engage). When reviewing for unusual activity, consider the following:

- For individual customers, whether the activity is consistent with available information (e.g., occupation, source of funds, and customer identification); and

- For business customers, whether the activity is consistent with examiner's knowledge of the business (e.g., type of business, size, location, and target market).

12. From the results of the sample, determine whether the MSB's manual or automated suspicious activity monitoring system effectively detects unusual or suspicious activity. Identify the underlying cause of any deficiencies in the monitoring systems (e.g., inappropriate filters, insufficient risk assessment, or inadequate decision-making).

13. For transactions identified as unusual, discuss the transactions with management and appropriate personnel involved in the transaction where applicable. Determine whether the personnel demonstrate knowledge of the customer and the unusual transactions. After examining the available facts, determine whether management knows of a reasonable explanation for the transactions or if an apparent reporting deficiency exists. Based on the response, the examiner may consider expanding the scope of the examination.

Additional MSB Examination Procedures for Issuance or Sale of Money Orders/Traveler's Checks Based on Risk

14. In the absence of adequate procedures to monitor suspicious activity, the examiner should sample daily transaction records and reports to determine if any potential suspicious activity occurred. Investigate whether appropriate procedures to report suspicious activity were followed.

15. For Principal MSBs that are issuers of money orders/traveler's checks, obtain the electronic records that list the serial number and the dollar amount of each money order/traveler's check that clears daily. This record should list the exact order the money orders/traveler's checks cleared through the MSB's account. From this record, examiners should analyze patterns for potentially suspicious transactions at $5,000 and greater. For example, the examiner should look for a customer purchasing money orders at various agent locations and then depositing them on the same day. An example of a pattern would be ten consecutive numbered money orders, each with a face amount of $500, clearing consecutively through the bank account.

16. Trace large block sales or large single-transaction sales of money orders/traveler's checks in the money order/traveler's check register or other similar reports to the records required for SAR-MSB reporting. A block sale involves the simultaneous sale of sequentially numbered money orders/traveler's checks for an amount at or

near the maximum dollar amount. The issuing company usually sets the maximum amount allowed for each money order/travelers check. The review should identify blocks of money orders/traveler's checks sold at or near the $2,000 threshold for potential suspicious activity. Request copies of money orders/traveler's checks for any questionable or potential suspicious transactions identified. (For agent MSBs, request that the agent MSB obtain copies of money orders/traveler's checks from the money order/traveler's check issuer.) Review the copies to determine whether there was unreported suspicious activity.

Additional Principal MSB Examination Procedures for Money Transmitters Based on Risk

17. Review transaction databases to determine if the MSB has filed SAR-MSBs in connection with any suspicious activity, and that reports were filed timely and correctly. Transaction databases can be sorted by sender name, recipient name, identification number, social security number, sender address, recipient address, sender phone number, and recipient phone number.

    • Perform an analysis for potential suspicious activity using the results of the various sorted transactions. For example, the examiner may scan groups of records for possible structured transactions occurring on the same day or over a period of several days. If a customer sends $6,000 at 5:00 p.m., then on the same day and at the same location at 5:10 p.m. sends $5,000 more, the customer could be structuring transactions. Examiners should be aware of these or similar situations and should be prepared to discuss potentially suspicious transactions with the BSA compliance officer.

    • When reviewing money transmitter transactions, note the telephone numbers used by the customer. A sender may give a false name and address but may use a correct telephone number (so that if the money cannot be delivered, the sender will be notified). Also, watch for repetitive senders' and/or recipients' names and addresses.

    • Discuss with management any patterns of potentially suspicious activity identified to determine whether suspicious activity was investigated and reported where appropriate. At a minimum, the activity should have been investigated and the decision not to file a SAR-MSB explained.

Additional Examination Procedures for Currency Dealers or Exchangers Based on Risk

18. Select dates within the period and reconcile the transaction vouchers, daily transaction log, client ledger, and monthly and annual summary sheets. Analyze the summary and transaction records for cash in and cash out for transactions conducted by the currency dealer or exchanger. All large or unusual items should be reviewed to determine whether potential suspicious activity was investigated and reported where appropriate. At a minimum, the activity should have been investigated, and the decision not to file a SAR-MSB should have been explained.

Evaluating the MSB's Compliance with Suspicious Activity Reporting Requirements

19. If a determination is made that records and reporting procedures are inadequate, or were destroyed or not maintained, the examiner should:

    • Expand the scope of the BSA examination; and

    • Document all problem areas and findings in the workpapers.

20. Based on the risks identified by the examiner during the examination, the examiner may consider reviewing all financial services offered by the MSB to determine if transactions are being structured by using a variety of financial services.

21. On the basis of examination procedures completed, including transaction testing, form a conclusion about the ability of policies, procedures, and processes to meet regulatory requirements associated with monitoring, detecting, and reporting suspicious activity.

Foreign Bank and Financial Accounts Reporting — Overview

Objective: *Assess the MSB's compliance with statutory and regulatory requirements for the reporting of foreign bank and financial accounts.*

Citizens and residents of the United States, and persons[75] (including MSBs) in, and doing business in, the United States that have financial interest in or signature authority over a bank account, securities account, or any other financial account in a foreign country, must file a Report of Foreign Bank and Financial Accounts (FBAR), Treasury Department Form TD F 90-22.1, if the aggregate value of these financial accounts exceeds $10,000 at any time during the calendar year. An MSB must file this form with respect to its own accounts that meet this definition. In addition, the MSB may be obligated to file these forms for customer accounts in which it has a financial interest or over which it has signature authority. The FBAR must be filed with the IRS on or before June 30 of each calendar year, for foreign financial accounts exceeding $10,000 that were maintained at any time during the previous calendar year.

If an MSB has a financial interest in or signature or other authority over foreign financial accounts and must file a Report of Foreign Bank and Financial Accounts (FBAR), Treasury Department Form TD F 90-22.1, records of the accounts must be retained if the aggregate value of the accounts exceeds $10,000 at any time during the calendar year. The records must contain:

- The name in which each account is maintained;

- The number or other designation of such account;

- The name and address of the foreign bank or other person with whom such account is maintained;

- The account type; and

- The maximum value of each such account during the reporting period.[76]

An MSB must retain records of these accounts (if any exist) for five years.[77]

---

75. As defined in 31 CFR 103.11(z), the term "person" means an individual, a corporation, a partnership, a trust or estate, a joint stock company, an association, a syndicate, joint venture or other unincorporated organization or group, an Indian Tribe (as that term is defined in the Indian Gaming Regulatory Act), and all entities cognizable as legal personalities.
76. 31 CFR 103.32.
77. 31 CFR 103.38(d) and 31 CFR 103.32.

Examination Procedures
Foreign Bank and Financial Accounts

1. Determine whether the MSB or its owners have a business or personal financial interest in or signature authority over any bank, securities, or other financial accounts in a foreign country, or whether the MSB is otherwise required to file a Report of Foreign Bank and Financial Accounts (FBAR) (TD F 90-22.1).

2. Review copies of FBARs and supporting documentation for accuracy and completeness. The Web CBRS database should also be checked to verify that the reports were actually filed.

3. On the basis of examination procedures completed, form a conclusion about the adequacy of policies, procedures, and processes to meet regulatory requirements associated with FBARs.

International Transportation of Currency or Monetary Instruments Reporting — Overview

Objective: *Assess the MSB's compliance with statutory and regulatory requirements for the reporting of international shipments of currency or monetary instruments.*

Each person[78] (including an MSB) who physically transports, mails, or ships currency or monetary instruments in excess of $10,000 at one time out of or into the United States (and each person who causes such transportation, mailing, or shipment) must file a Report of International Transportation of Currency or Monetary Instruments (CMIR) (FinCEN Form 105).[79] A CMIR must be filed with the appropriate Bureau of Customs and Border Protection officer or with the Commissioner of Customs and Border Protection at the time of entry into or departure from the United States. When a person receives currency or monetary instruments in an amount exceeding $10,000 at one time that has been shipped from any place outside the United States, a CMIR must be filed with the appropriate Bureau of Customs and Border Protection officer or with the Commissioner of Customs and Border Protection within 15 days of receipt of the currency or instruments (unless a report has already been filed).

Management should implement appropriate policies, procedures, and processes for CMIR filing. Management should review the international transportation of currency and monetary instruments and determine whether a customer's activity is usual and customary for the customer's type of business. If not, management should consider filing a Suspicious Activity Report.

MSBs must keep a record of each transaction that results in the receipt (except from a bank) or the transfer of more that $10,000 in currency or monetary instruments to or from any person, account or place outside the United States.[80]

---

78. As defined in 31 CFR 103.11(z), the term "person" means an individual, a corporation, a partnership, a trust or estate, a joint stock company, an association, a syndicate, joint venture or other unincorporated organization or group, an Indian Tribe (as that term is defined in the Indian Gaming Regulatory Act), and all entities cognizable as legal personalities.

79. The obligation to file the CMIR is solely on the person who transports, mails, ships or receives, or causes or attempts to transport, mail, ship, or receive. No other person is under any obligation to file a CMIR. Thus, if a customer walks into the bank and declares that he or she has received or transported currency in an aggregate amount exceeding $10,000 from a place outside the United States and wishes to deposit the currency into his or her account, the bank is under no obligation to file a CMIR on the customer's behalf (Treasury Administrative Ruling 88-2).

80. 31 CFR 103.33(b) and (c).

Examination Procedures International
Transportation of Currency or Monetary Instruments Reporting

1. Determine whether the MSB has (or has caused to be) physically transported, mailed, or shipped currency or other monetary instruments in excess of $10,000, at one time, into or out of the United States, or whether the MSB has received currency or other monetary instruments in excess of $10,000, at one time, that have been physically transported, mailed, or shipped into the United States.

2. If applicable, review the MSB's policies, procedures, and processes for filing a Report of International Transportation of Currency or Monetary Instruments (CMIR) (FinCEN Form 105) for each shipment of currency or other monetary instruments in excess of $10,000 out of or into the United States unless an exception from CMIR reporting applies).[81] Determine if the MSB's policies, procedures, and processes are appropriate to ensure compliance (e.g., adequate review process, transaction monitoring, and appropriate segregation of duties).

Additional Examination Procedures Based on Risk

3. Based on a risk assessment, prior examination reports, and a review of the MSB's prior examination findings, determine if the MSB has filed CMIRs for required transactions greater than $10,000. Select a sample of transactions conducted and determine whether the MSB appropriately completed and submitted CMIR forms. Check the Web CBRS database to verify that the reports were actually filed. Verify information reported against information collected on transaction databases, identification records, other transaction records, and interviews with personnel. Information reported should be consistent.

4. Determine through review of reports and transaction records if CMIRs filed by the MSB were been filed within the required timeframe.

Evaluating the MSB's Compliance with International Transportation of Currency or Monetary Instruments Reporting

5. On the basis of examination procedures completed, form a conclusion about the ability of the MSB's policies, procedures, and processes to meet regulatory requirements associated with CMIRs.

---

81. See 31 CFR 103.23(c) for exceptions to CMIR reporting.

Developing Conclusions and Finalizing the Examination — Overview

Objective: *Formulate conclusions, communicate findings to management, prepare report comments, develop an appropriate supervisory response, and close the examination.*

In the final phase of the BSA examination, the examiner should assemble all findings from the completed examination procedures. From those findings, the examiner should develop and document conclusions about the AML program's adequacy and aggregate risk profile of the MSB; discuss preliminary conclusions with management; present these conclusions in a written format for inclusion in the report of examination; and, determine and document what regulatory response, if any, is appropriate.

Examiner Determination of the MSB's BSA/AML Aggregate Money Laundering Risk Profile

The examiner should assess whether the controls of the MSB's AML program are appropriate to manage and mitigate its money laundering risks. Through this process, the examiner should determine an aggregate risk profile for the MSB. This aggregate risk profile should take into consideration the risk assessment developed either by the MSB or by the examiner and should factor in the adequacy of the AML program. Examiners should determine whether the MSB's AML program is adequate to appropriately mitigate the money laundering risks, based on the risk assessment. The existence of money laundering risk within the aggregate risk profile should not be criticized as long as the MSB's AML program adequately identifies, measures, monitors, and controls this risk as part of a deliberate risk mitigation strategy. When the risks are not appropriately controlled, examiners should communicate to MSB management and the board of directors, where applicable, the need to mitigate money laundering risk. Examiners should document deficiencies.

In formulating a written conclusion, the examiner does not need to discuss every procedure performed during the examination. During discussions with management about examination conclusions, examiners should include discussions of both strengths and weaknesses of the MSB's BSA compliance. Examiners should document all relevant determinations and conclusions.

Examination Procedures
Developing Conclusions and Finalizing the Examination

1. Accumulate all pertinent findings from the BSA examination procedures performed. Evaluate the thoroughness and reliability of any risk assessment conducted by the MSB. Determine whether the AML program is effectively monitored and supervised in relation to the MSB's risk profile as determined by the risk assessment. The examiner should ascertain if the AML program is effective in mitigating the MSB's overall risk. After analyzing the MSB's BSA/AML policies, procedures, internal controls, monitoring, and reporting processes, the BSA examiner should draw conclusions as to the adequacy of the MSB's AML program.

   - Determine whether the program has been adequately implemented.

   - Determine whether there has been a systemic breakdown of internal controls or lack of adherence to policy procedures to assure compliance.

   - Determine whether the MSB was aware of any problems in its AML program, and whether it took corrective action.

   - Assess whether any breakdowns in the program could place the MSB at increased risk of being used by customers to launder money or commit other types of financial crimes.

   - Identify any weaknesses or deficiencies in the program that could or did result in failures to correctly file required CTRs, other required reports, and/or failure to comply with the BSA recordkeeping and record retention requirements.

   - Determine whether senior management and the board of directors (if applicable) are aware of BSA regulatory requirements; effectively oversee BSA compliance; and commit, as necessary, to corrective actions (e.g., independent reviews and regulatory examinations).

   - Determine whether BSA/AML policies, procedures, and processes are adequate to ensure compliance with applicable laws and regulations and appropriately address high-risk operations (products, services, customers, geographic locations, etc.).

   - Evaluate whether internal controls ensure compliance with the BSA and provide sufficient risk management, especially for high-risk products, services, customers, geographic locations, etc.

   - Determine if independent testing is appropriate and adequately tests for compliance with required laws, regulations, and policies.

   - Determine whether the designated person responsible for coordinating and monitoring day-to-day compliance is competent and has the necessary resources.

- Determine whether personnel are sufficiently trained to be able to adhere to legal, regulatory, and policy requirements as appropriate, based on their job duties.

- Evaluate whether information and communication policies, procedures, and processes are adequate and accurate.

2. Determine the underlying cause(s) of policy, procedure, or process deficiencies, if identified. These deficiencies can be the result of a number of factors, including, but not limited to, the following:

   - Management has not assessed, or has not accurately assessed, the MSB's money laundering risks;

   - Management is unaware of relevant issues;

   - Management is unwilling or unable to create or enhance policies, procedures, and processes;

   - Management or employees disregard established policies, procedures, and processes;

   - Management or employees are unaware of or misunderstand regulatory requirements, policies, procedures, or processes;

   - High-risk operations (with respect to products, services, customers, geographic locations, etc.) have grown faster than the capabilities of the AML program; or

   - Changes in internal policies, procedures, and processes are poorly communicated.

3. Determine whether deficiencies or violations were previously identified by management or the examiner, or were only identified as a result of this examination.

4. Identify actions needed to correct outstanding deficiencies or violations, as appropriate, including the possibility of, among other things, requiring the MSB to conduct an appropriate risk assessment or implement appropriate policies, procedures, or internal controls, or taking formal enforcement action against the MSB.

Supporting Workpaper Documentation

5. The examiner should obtain the following documentation for each example of the following violations that is uncovered:

   - Reporting – The date of the transaction, the amount, the individuals involved, and a detailed statement regarding the violation, including copies of source documents such as cash in/out slips, control registers, teller cash proofs that support the violation, and documentation of management's response to the violation. For reporting violations, the examiner should obtain documentation of management's response to the violation.

- Recordkeeping – The details of the specific records that were not maintained or were inadequate, including management's response to the violation.

Preparing the BSA Report of Examination

6. Develop a conclusion regarding the adequacy of the MSB's AML program. Discuss the effectiveness of each of the elements of the MSB's AML program. Indicate whether the AML program meets all the regulatory requirements by providing the following:

    - A system of internal controls;

    - Independent testing for compliance;

    - A specific person to coordinate and monitor the AML program; and

    - Training of appropriate personnel.

7. Ensure that workpapers are prepared in sufficient detail to support issues discussed in the report of examination (ROE). Written comments should cover areas or subjects pertinent to the examiner's findings and conclusions. All significant findings should be included in the ROE. To the extent that items are discussed in the workpapers but not the ROE, the examiner should ensure that the workpapers thoroughly and adequately document each review, as well as any other aspect of the MSB's AML program that merits attention but may not rise to the level of being included in the ROE.

8. As applicable, the examiner should prepare a discussion of the following items:

    - Describe the MSB's commitment to BSA compliance. Consider whether management has the following:

        ▪ A strong AML program fully supported by the board of directors.

        ▪ A requirement that senior management and the board of directors (if applicable) are kept informed of BSA compliance efforts, examination reports, any compliance failures, and the status of corrective actions.

    - Describe whether the MSB's policies, procedures, and processes for SAR-MSB filings meet the regulatory requirements and are effective.

    - Describe whether the MSB's policies, procedures, and processes for large currency transactions meet the requirements of 31 CFR 103.22 and are effective.

    - Describe whether the MSB's funds transfer policies, procedures, and processes meet the requirements of 31 CFR 103.33(f) and (g).

    - Describe the MSB's recordkeeping policies, procedures, and processes. Indicate whether they meet the requirements of 31 CFR 103.

Closing Conference

9. Hold a closing conference to discuss all identified and verified violations, including deficiencies in policies, procedures, internal controls, and AML programs. The examiner should advise the entity of any deficiencies in its policies, procedures, internal controls, compliance program, recordkeeping, and reporting requirements. The examiner should provide the MSB with a list of potential violations and deficiencies. Any additional documents or information provided by the MSB in response to the list provided should be reviewed and a determination should be made as to whether any items should be removed from the list of violations. Examiners should provide the MSB with feedback to help the MSB avoid future violations. The examiner should document the date of the closing conference, who attended, and the nature of the discussions during the closing conference.

Handling Initial Notification of and Response to Violations

10. After documenting the potential violations, the examiner should provide a list of the violations to the MSB and solicit a written explanation for each of the violations identified. The list should include:

- Date of the transaction;
- Customer name;
- Account number (if any);
- Check number (if any);
- Amount involved in transaction; and
- Description of the transaction.

11. Review any additional documents or information provided by the MSB in response and determine whether any items should be removed from the list of violations.

APPENDIX A – BACKGROUND

Over the years, Congress has passed many laws to combat money laundering. Perhaps the most significant of these are the reporting, recordkeeping, and anti-money laundering provisions of the Currency and Foreign Transactions Reporting Act, the Money Laundering Control Act of 1986, the Anti-Drug Abuse Act of 1988, the Annunzio-Wylie Act of 1992, the Money Laundering Suppression Act of 1994, the Money Laundering and Financial Crimes Strategy Act of 1998 and the USA PATRIOT Act of 2001. Collectively, these provisions are popularly known as the Bank Secrecy Act.

The **Currency and Foreign Transactions Reporting Act** (Title II of P.L. 91-508) was designed to:

- Prevent tax evasion and provide tools to fight organized crime.

- Create an investigative "paper trail" for large currency transactions by establishing reporting standards and requirements (e.g., the Currency Transaction Report requirement).

- Require financial institutions to verify the identity of customers and keep certain basic records of customer transactions, including cancelled checks, debits, signature cards, and statements of account.

- Impose civil and criminal penalties for noncompliance with its reporting requirements.

- Improve detection and investigation of criminal, tax, and regulatory violations.

The **Money Laundering Control Act** of 1986 (Title I, Subtitle H of P.L. 99-570), part of the Anti-Drug Abuse Act of 1986, made money laundering a federal crime. It created three new criminal offenses for money laundering activities by, through, or to a financial institution. These offenses are:

- Knowingly helping launder money derived from criminal activity.

- Knowingly engaging in a transaction of more than $10,000 that involves property or funds derived from criminal activity (including being willfully blind to the criminal source of the funds).

- Structuring transactions to evade BSA reporting requirements.

The **Anti-Drug Abuse Act** of 1988 (P.L. 100-690) reinforced anti-money laundering efforts in several ways. The Act:

- Significantly increases civil and criminal penalties for money laundering and other BSA violations, including forfeiture of any property, real or personal, involved in a transaction or attempted transaction in violation of laws relating to money laundering, structuring transactions, or the filing of Currency Transaction Reports.

- Requires strict identification and recording of currency purchases of certain monetary instruments, including money orders and traveler's checks between $3,000 and $10,000, inclusive.

- Permits the Department of the Treasury to require certain financial institutions in specific geographic or "target" areas to file additional BSA reports of currency transactions in amounts less than $10,000 by use of Geographic Targeting Orders.

- Directs the Department of the Treasury to negotiate bilateral international agreements covering the recording of large U.S. currency transactions and the sharing of such information.

- Increases the criminal sanction for tax evasion when money from criminal activity is involved.

The **Annunzio-Wylie Anti-Money Laundering Act** of 1992 (Title XV of P.L. 102-550) strengthened penalties for financial institutions found guilty of money laundering. Annunzio-Wylie required the Secretary of the Treasury to:

- Adopt a rule requiring all financial institutions, both banks and non-banks (including MSBs), to maintain records of domestic and international funds transfers, which can be used in law enforcement investigations.

- Establish a BSA Advisory Group (BSAAG), comprised of representatives from the Department of the Treasury and Department of Justice, Office of National Drug Control Policy, and other interested persons and financial institutions, including MSBs. The BSAAG, established in 1994, meets twice per year and informs representatives of the financial services industry about new regulatory developments and how reported information is used.

Annunzio-Wylie also permitted the Secretary of the Treasury to:

- Require any financial institution, or any financial institution employee, to report suspicious transactions relevant to any possible violation of law or regulation.

- Require any financial institution to adopt an anti-money laundering program.

In addition, Annunzio-Wylie:

- Makes it illegal for a financial institution, or an employee of a financial institution, to disclose to anyone involved in a suspicious transaction when the financial institution has filed a Suspicious Activity Report (SAR) on the transaction.

- Protects any financial institution, and any director, officer, employee, or agent of a financial institution, from civil liability for reporting suspicious activity.

- Makes it a federal crime to operate an illegal money transmitting business (i.e., operating a money transmitting business without a state license in a state where such license is required under state law).

The **Money Laundering Suppression Act (MLSA)** of 1994 (Title IV of P.L. 103-325) specifically addressed MSBs. The MLSA:

- Requires each MSB to be registered by an owner or controlling person of the MSB.

- Requires every MSB to maintain a list of businesses authorized to act as agents in connection with selling the financial services offered by the MSB.

- Makes operating an unregistered MSB a federal crime.

- Recommends that states adopt uniform laws applicable to MSBs.

The **Money Laundering and Financial Crimes Strategy Act** of 1998 (P.L. 105-310) requires:

- The President, acting through the Secretary of the Treasury and in coordination with the Attorney General, to develop a national strategy for combating money laundering and related financial crimes and to submit such strategy each February 1st to Congress.

- The Secretary of the Treasury, upon consultation with the Attorney General, to designate certain areas—by geographical area, industry, sector, or institution—as being vulnerable to money laundering and related financial crimes. (Certain areas were subsequently designated as High Intensity Financial Crime Areas (HIFCAs)).

The **USA PATRIOT Act** of 2001 (Title III of P.L. 107-56),[82] requires:

- Establishment of anti-money laundering compliance programs by all financial institutions. At a minimum, each program must include: policies, procedures, and controls, designation of a compliance officer, training, and an independent audit function.

- Establishment of a confidential communication system between government and the financial services industry.

- Implementation of customer identification procedures for new accounts.

- Enhanced due diligence for correspondent and private banking accounts maintained for non-U.S. persons.

- Establishment of a highly secure network by FinCEN for electronic filing of BSA reports.

---

82. The full title is the Uniting and Strengthening America by Providing Appropriate Tools Required to Intercept and Obstruct Terrorism (USA PATRIOT) Act of 2001, and Title III of the USA PATRIOT Act is the International Money Laundering Abatement and Financial Anti-Terrorism Act of 2001. Financial institutions and their regulators, however, commonly refer to Title III as the USA PATRIOT Act.

Role of Federal and State Government Agencies in the BSA

Certain government agencies play a critical role in implementing BSA regulations, developing examination guidance, ensuring compliance with the BSA, and enforcing the BSA. These agencies include FinCEN, the federal bank regulatory agencies (Board of Governors of the Federal Reserve System, Federal Deposit Insurance Corporation, National Credit Union Administration, Office of the Comptroller of the Currency, Office of Thrift Supervision), the Securities and Exchange Commission, the Internal Revenue Service, and the Commodity Futures Trading Commission. Although the BSA is not directly enforced by state agencies, the state agencies are charged with enforcing state statutes and regulations that apply to MSBs, which may impose requirements that overlap with those of the BSA. Internationally there are various intergovernmental organizations (such as the FATF) that support the fight against money laundering and terrorist financing. Two Treasury bureaus are of primary importance in connection with the regulation of MSBs for BSA compliance.

FinCEN

The BSA authorizes the Secretary of the Treasury to require financial institutions to establish AML programs, file certain reports, and keep certain records of transactions. Certain BSA provisions have been extended to cover not only traditional depository institutions, such as banks, savings associations, and credit unions, but also non-bank financial institutions, such as MSBs, casinos, broker/dealers in securities, futures commission merchants, mutual funds, insurance companies, and operators of credit card systems.

FinCEN, a bureau of the Treasury Department, is the delegated administrator of the BSA. In this capacity, FinCEN issues regulations and interpretive guidance, provides outreach to regulated industries, supports the examination functions performed by federal and state agencies, and pursues civil enforcement actions when warranted. FinCEN relies on the Internal Revenue Service to examine MSBs and certain other non-bank financial institutions for compliance with the BSA. FinCEN's other significant responsibilities include providing investigative case support to law enforcement, identifying and communicating financial crime trends and patterns, and fostering international cooperation with its counterparts worldwide.

Internal Revenue Service

The Internal Revenue Service (IRS), which is another bureau of the Department of the Treasury, plays a significant role in national anti-money laundering efforts. The IRS derives its BSA examination authority from 31 CFR 103.56(b)(8). This regulation delegates to the Commissioner of the IRS the authority to examine certain non-bank financial institutions for compliance with BSA requirements. Furthermore, Treasury Directive 15-41 delegates to the Commissioner of the IRS the authority to conduct BSA examinations of certain non-bank financial institutions to assure compliance.

Money Laundering and Terrorist Financing

Compliance with the BSA safeguards the U.S. financial system and the financial institutions that make up that system from financial crime, including money laundering, terrorist financing, and other illicit financial transactions. Financial organizations must develop, implement, and maintain effective AML programs that address the ever-changing strategies of money launderers and terrorists who attempt to gain access to the U.S. financial system. A sound AML program is critical in deterring and preventing these types of activities at, or through, MSBs and other financial institutions.

Money is "laundered" to conceal illegal activity, including the crimes that generate the money itself, such as drug trafficking. Money laundering conceals the source of illegal proceeds so that the money can be used without detection of its criminal source.

Financial institutions — including MSBs — may be either witting or unwitting participants in money laundering activities. Banks have been major targets in money laundering operations because they provide a variety of services, including funds transmittals and the sale of cashier's checks and traveler's checks, which can be used to conceal the source of illicit proceeds.

Similarly, criminals use MSBs — establishments that provide money orders, traveler's checks, money transfers, check cashing, or currency exchange — to hide or disguise the origin of funds derived from illegal activity. In order to protect themselves and to support national and international efforts against financial crime, it is important that MSBs know how money laundering schemes can operate.

Money Laundering

Money laundering is motivated by the desire to make illegally obtained money available for new uses. Money laundering can be a complex process. It involves three different, and sometimes overlapping, stages:

Placement - introducing illegally obtained money into the financial system or the retail economy by a deposit or purchase. Illegally obtained money is most vulnerable to detection and seizure during placement.

Layering - separating the illegally obtained money from its criminal sources by layering it through a series of financial transactions, which makes it difficult to trace the money back to its original source.

Integration - moving the proceeds into seemingly legitimate forms. Integration may include the purchase of automobiles, businesses, real estate, etc.

An important factor connecting the three stages of this process is the "paper trail" generated by financial transactions. Criminals try to avoid leaving this "paper trail" by avoiding reporting and recordkeeping requirements.

Money launderers may try to avoid reporting and recordkeeping requirements by coercing or bribing employees not to file proper reports or complete required records, by creating apparently legitimate "front" businesses to open accounts or establish preferred customer relationships, or by "structuring" transactions to keep them below reporting thresholds.

Terrorist Financing

The motivation behind terrorist financing is ideological as opposed to profit-seeking. Terrorism is intended to intimidate a population or to compel a government or an international organization to do or abstain from doing a specific act through the threat of violence. Terrorist groups develop sources of funding that are relatively mobile to ensure that funds can be used to satisfy the material and logistical requirements to commit terrorist acts.

Terrorists may finance their activities with funds from either unlawful or legitimate sources. Unlawful activities, such as extortion, kidnapping, and narcotics trafficking, may be a source of funding. Other possible activities include smuggling, fraud, theft, robbery, identity theft, use of conflict diamonds[83], and improper use of charitable or relief funds. In the last case, donors may have no knowledge that their donations have been diverted to support terrorist causes. Terrorists' use of unlawful sources of funds means that money laundering is often a vital component of terrorist financing.

Other legitimate sources have also been found to provide terrorist organizations with funding; these legitimate funding sources are a key difference between terrorist financiers and traditional criminal organizations. In addition to charitable donations, legitimate sources include foreign government sponsors, business operations, and personal employment.

Although the motivations of traditional money launderers and terrorist financiers differ, the actual methods used to fund terrorist operations can be the same as or similar to those methods used by other criminals that launder funds. For example, terrorist

---

83. Conflict diamonds originate from areas controlled by forces or factions opposed to legitimate and internationally recognized governments and are used to fund military action in opposition to those governments, or in contravention of the decisions of the United Nations Security Council (www.un.org/peace/africa/Diamond.html).

---

financiers may use currency smuggling; structured deposits or withdrawals from institution accounts; purchases of various types of monetary instruments; credit, debit, or stored value cards; and funds transfers. Funding for terrorist attacks does not always require large sums of money, and the associated transactions may not be complex.

Criminal Penalties for Money Laundering, Terrorist Financing, and Violations of the BSA

Penalties for money laundering and terrorist financing can be severe. A person convicted of money laundering can face up to 20 years in prison and a fine of up to $500,000.[84] Any property involved in a transaction or traceable to the proceeds of the criminal activity, including property such as loan collateral, personal property, and, under certain conditions, entire institution accounts (even if some of the money in the account is legitimate), may be subject to forfeiture. Pursuant to various statutes, financial institutions and individuals may incur criminal and civil liability for violating AML and terrorist financing laws. For instance, pursuant to 18 USC 1956 and 1957, the Department of Justice may bring criminal actions for money laundering that may include criminal fines, imprisonment, and forfeiture actions.[85] In addition, financial institutions risk losing their charters and licenses.

Moreover, there are criminal penalties for willful violations of the BSA and its implementing regulations under 31 USC 5322, failing to register a money transmitting business under 18 USC 1960, and structuring transactions to evade BSA reporting requirements under 31 USC 5324(d). For example, a person, including a financial institution employee, willfully violating the BSA or its implementing regulations is subject to a criminal fine of up to $250,000 or five years in prison, or both.[86] A person who commits such a violation while violating another U.S. law, or engaging in a pattern of criminal activity, is subject to a fine of up to $500,000 or ten years in prison, or both.[87] A financial institution that violates certain BSA provisions, including 31 USC 5318(i) or (j), or special measures imposed under 31 USC 5318A, faces criminal money penalties up to the lesser of $1 million or twice the value of the transaction.[88]

---

84. 18 USC 1956.

85. 18 USC 981 and 982.

86. 31 USC 5322(a).

87. 31 USC 5322(b).

88. 31 USC 5322(d).

Civil Penalties for Violations of the BSA

Pursuant to 31 USC 5321, FinCEN can bring civil money penalty actions for violations of the BSA. Moreover, in addition to criminal and civil money penalty actions taken against them, individuals may be prosecuted under their state licensing statutes for violations of the AML laws under Title 31 of the U.S. Code. Information on all of these actions is publicly available.

APPENDIX B – BSA LAWS AND REGULATIONS

A copy of the current BSA Laws and Regulations can be found on the internet at http://www.fincen.gov/statutes_regs/bsa/

31 CFR 103 — **"Financial Recordkeeping and Reporting of Currency and Foreign Transactions"**

Sets forth FinCEN regulations that promulgate the BSA Select provisions described below.

31 CFR 103.11 — **"Meaning of Terms"**

Sets forth the definitions used throughout 31 CFR Part 103.

31 CFR 103.20 — **"Reports by Money Services Businesses of Suspicious Transactions."**

Sets forth the requirements for money services businesses to report suspicious transactions of $2,000 or more. Includes 31 CFR 103.20(d), which states that the requirements for money orders or traveler's checks sold or processed shall only apply to transactions aggregating more than $5,000.

31 CFR 103.22 — **"Reports of Transactions in Currency"**

Sets forth the requirements for financial institutions to report currency transactions in excess of $10,000.

31 CFR 103.23 — **"Reports of Transportation of Currency or Monetary Instruments"**

Sets forth the requirements for filing a Currency or Monetary Instruments Report.

31 CFR 103.24 — **"Reports of Foreign Financial Accounts"**

Sets forth the requirement that each person having a financial account in a foreign country file a report with the Internal Revenue Service annually.

31 CFR 103.27 — **"Filing of Reports"**

Filing and recordkeeping requirements for Currency Transaction Reports (CTRs), Report of International Transportation of Currency or Monetary Instruments (CMIR), and Report of Foreign Bank and Financial Accounts (FBAR).

31 CFR 103.28 — "Identification Required"

Sets forth the requirement that financial institutions verify the identity of persons conducting currency transactions in excess of $10,000.

31 CFR 103.29 — "Purchases of Bank Checks and Drafts, Cashier's Checks, Money Orders, and Traveler's Checks"

Sets forth the requirements that financial institutions maintain records relating to purchases of bank checks and drafts, cashier's checks, money orders, and traveler's checks in currency in amounts between $3,000 and $10,000.

31 CFR 103.32 — "Records to Be Made and Retained by Persons Having Financial Interests in Foreign Financial Accounts"

Sets forth the requirement that persons having a financial account in a foreign country maintain records relating to foreign financial bank accounts reported on an FBAR.

31 CFR 103.33 — "Records to Be Made and Retained by Financial Institutions"

Sets forth recordkeeping and retrieval requirements for financial institutions, including funds transfer recordkeeping and transmittal requirements.

31 CFR 103.37 — Additional Records to Be Made and Retained by Currency Dealers or Exchangers"

Sets forth additional recordkeeping requirements for currency dealers or exchangers.

31 CFR 103.38 — "Nature of Records and Retention Period"

Sets forth acceptable forms of records required to be kept and establishes a five-year record retention requirement.

31 CFR 103.41 — "Registration of Money Services Businesses"

Requirements for money services businesses to register with FinCEN.

31 CFR 103.56 – "Enforcement"

Sets forth the overall authority for enforcement and compliance of the Bank Secrecy Act.

31 CFR 103.57 — "Civil Penalty"

Sets forth potential civil penalties for willful or negligent violations of 31 CFR Part 103.

31 CFR 103.59 — "Criminal Penalty"

Sets forth potential criminal penalties for willful violations of 31 CFR Part 103.

31 CFR 103.63 — "Structured Transactions"

Prohibits the structuring of transactions to avoid the currency reporting requirement.

31 CFR 103.100 — "Information Sharing Between Federal Law Enforcement Agencies and Financial Institutions"

Establishes procedures and information sharing between federal law enforcement and financial institutions to deter money laundering and terrorist activity.

31 CFR 103.110 — "Voluntary Information Sharing Among Financial Institutions"

Establishes procedures for voluntary information sharing among financial institutions to deter money laundering and terrorist activity.

31 CFR 103.125 — "Anti-Money Laundering Program Requirements for Money Services Businesses"

Establishes the statutory requirement that a money services business must develop, implement and maintain an effective AML program that is reasonably designed to prevent money laundering and terrorist financing.

APPENDIX C – RISK MATRIX

The example risk matrix is an examination tool for examiners to use when assessing the risks of the MSB under examination.

Below are some examples of risk characteristics a BSA examiner could encounter during a BSA examination. These examples are not exhaustive. They provide an illustration of how the business operations and control environment can affect the risk of BSA non-compliance.

		LOWER RISK	*HIGHER RISK*
AML COMPLIANCE PROGRAM		The MSB has a written risk assessment of the financial services it offers to its customers.	The MSB has not performed a risk assessment.
		The MSB has a written AML program tailored to its risk assessment. The AML program has been implemented and is reasonably designed to ensure BSA compliance.	The MSB does not have an AML program or has not implemented the AML program.
		The AML program defines the duties of all the MSB's personnel, including the BSA compliance officer and personnel responsible for preparing BSA Reports and transactions.	The AML program does not define the duties of the MSB's personnel.
		The AML program addresses specific risks at the agent level	The AML program has not been modified to identify specific risks at agent level.
		The AML program covers all financial services offered by the MSB.	The AML program in place does not address all financial services that the entity provides.
		An independent review has been conducted, and the MSB has implemented the recommendations from the review.	An independent review has not been conducted, or the MSB has not implemented the recommendations from the independent review.
		The MSB has a documented BSA/AML training program, including dates and names of training provided to appropriate personnel.	The MSB does not provide continuous BSA/AML training to appropriate personnel.
		The author of the compliance program, policies, procedures and training does not conduct the independent review for the MSB.	The author of the compliance program, policies, procedures and training also conducts the independent review for the MSB.

	LOWER RISK	*HIGHER RISK*
INTERNAL CONTROL	The internal control procedures of the MSB provide for separation of duties, including custody of assets and recordkeeping functions.	The MSB does not have written procedures for the separation of duties.
	Different staff than those conducting the transactions perform transactional reviews and BSA report preparation.	The same staff conducting the financial transactions prepares, reviews, and files required BSA reports.
	Management documents oversight duties, including decisions made to file or not file BSA reports.	The MSB does not document its oversight duties and decisions.
	Error recognition computer software is in place to prevent the completion of a customer transaction when invalid or illogical data is input.	Employees can override input fields with invalid or illogical data entries when completing customer transactions.
	Electronic data is secure. A Business Continuation Plan is in place to provide back-ups for all records.	Electronic data is not secure. No plans are in place for emergency data restoration.
	The MSB has posted its fees for the public to see.	The MSB has special rates for different types of transactions or special customers that are not available to the general public.
	Transactional limitations are in place. Transactions in excess of limitation will not process without management or BSA compliance officer approval.	Transactional limits are not in place. For example, the use of multiple money orders/traveler's checks to purchase product or service is typical.
		Transactional limitations do not meet customer needs, yet affected customers continue to use the MSB services.
		Transactional limitations enforced by 3rd party, but no provision at retail level to prevent multiple transactions that could circumvent the limitations.
	Minimal employee turnover.	Frequent employee turnover.

	LOWER RISK	*HIGHER RISK*
INTERNAL CONTROL	MSB employs automated systems to assist in identifying potential money laundering and/or terrorist financing.	MSB relies solely on paper documents.
		MSB relies solely on automated reporting systems. Frontline employees do not initiate suspicious activity reports.
	Entity has controls in place to prevent losses or potential money laundering. These may include making copies of checks or other funds received from the customer, or creating detailed records of certain transactions.	New employees can conduct transactions of any amount before they receive BSA/AML training.
	Formal transaction system in place requiring the use of a bank or other formal system to perform transactions.	Hawalas and any other 'informal' transaction system.
	MSB obtains the majority of the currency needed from its bank.	MSB receives the currency needed to provide the financial service from sources other than its bank.
BUSINESS PRACTICES	Transactional dollar limitations are in place. Transactions in excess of limitation will not process.	No transaction limitations, or no system lock-out when processing transactions greater than the established limit.
	An organized and complete recordkeeping system is utilized.	No organized recordkeeping system is used.
	The MSB separates the financial and bookkeeping activities of the MSB from his/her other business.	The MSB does not separate the financial and bookkeeping activities of the MSB from his/her other business.
	The management of the MSB is aware of the BSA, sound businesses practices (such as cash flow management) and accounting controls and procedures.	The management of the MSB is unaware of the BSA, sound businesses practices (such as cash flow management) and accounting controls and procedures.
	MSB uses bank checks to pay expenses.	MSB pays expenses of business with cash.
	MSB charges check cashing fees.	MSB does not charge for check cashing fee.

	LOWER RISK	*HIGHER RISK*
CUSTOMERS	The customer base is stable and has been for several years. For example, most of the customers are employees from a large employer located near the MSB. The MSB cashes individuals' checks, which require less currency to be kept on hand. The value of individual transactions as well as total volume are within expected range for customer base. Customers transmit funds to countries that have strong money laundering oversight and controls.	The customer base is volatile in terms of few repeat customers; transaction volume is unpredictable, and subject to large swings between time periods. For example, customers are self-employed. The MSB provides check cashing services to businesses that require large amounts of currency. The value of individual transactions as well as total volume are not within expected range for customer base. Customers transmit funds to countries that have poor money laundering oversight and controls.
AGENT CONTRACTS	The MSB has one Agent relationship. The Principal provides various services to the MSB including periodic on-site visits from the Principal's IT staff to provide support for any IT issues. The Principal also provides BSA/AML training materials, as well as an instructor for the agent's BSA/AML employee training seminars.	The MSB has more than one Agent relationship. The Principal does not monitor the day-to-day activities of its agents, provide up-to-date BSA/AML training, or perform internal reviews of its agents.

	LOWER RISK	*HIGHER RISK*
GEOGRAPHIC LOCATION	MSB is not located in a HIFCA or HIDTA area.	The MSB is located in a HIFCA and/or HIDTA area. Examiners should note that while the location of the MSB is an important factor, it is not the only factor. Determinations to the risk level of a particular MSB should involve an evaluation of all available information, including the nature and volume of the MSB's business and the control environment.
	The MSB provides services to the local community.	The MSB derives significant business from customers outside the community, e.g., transaction volume is greater than the local community would seem to be able to support, or customers are from distances outside the local community.
	The MSB is operating in high-traffic retail area.	The MSB is located in owner's personal residence or area that is not accessible to the public.
	No or minimal SAR-MSB activity seen when the area's location is researched on CBRS.	Significant SAR activity seen when the area's location is researched on CBRS.
	For MSBs with multiple locations, AML program and procedures address the risks at each location.	Entity with multiple locations, uses an AML program and procedures that do not consider the risks of all locations.

	LOWER RISK	*HIGHER RISK*
PRODUCTS AND SERVICES	Customers generally transmit funds and/or purchase money orders/traveler's checks with proceeds of payroll checks.	Customers generally pay for funds transmittals and/or purchase money orders/traveler's checks with currency.
		Customers generally pay for funds transmittals and/or purchase money orders/traveler's checks with proceeds from business checks or other monetary instruments.
	Products and services offered are those needed by the MSB's customer base.	One or more product or service that is needed by the MSB's customer base is not offered.
	MSB has a single Agent contract for each product or service.	MSB has multiple Agent contracts for one or more of the products and services offered.
		Products purchased by customers are shipped overseas.
		Transmittals of funds sent to intermediary countries that are known to be conduits to prohibited countries.
		Transactions are not done face-to-face.

APPENDIX D – SAMPLE REQUEST LETTER AND DOCUMENTS FOR MSBS

Sample Document Request for BSA Examination

This list is not exhaustive or required in all cases. An appropriate request will depend on the type of financial services provided by the MSB and will vary by the agency requesting documents for examination.

Please have available the following documents for our appointment:

1. Any written policy statements, procedures, etc. of the business as they relate to the reporting, recordkeeping, and structuring provisions of the Bank Secrecy Act (BSA). (This includes the AML Program)

2. Books and records required to be maintained pursuant to the BSA Regulations (31 CFR Part 103) and other records as required, for the period:

    a) Statements of accounts from banks, including paid checks, charges or other debit entry, memoranda, deposit slips and other credit memoranda;

    b) Daily and monthly work records, summaries and reconciliations needed to identify and reconstruct currency transactions with customers;

    c) Signature or customer cards or other documents containing the names of the customer, street addresses, and SSN/EIN;

    d) Copies of the daily, weekly, or monthly summary statements for money orders, traveler's checks, and funds transmittals;

    e) All records of money orders/traveler's checks sold (if applicable) between $3,000 and $10,000 that reflect the purchaser's name, address, social security number, and valid form of identification. (For example, the MSB may keep a log of money orders/traveler's checks sold that includes the required records.)

    f) Copies of all funds transmittal forms.

3. Copies of ALL the following BSA reports filed during the period involved:

    a) Form 104-Currency Transaction Report (CTR)

    b) Form 105/Report of International Transaction of Currency or Monetary Instruments (CMIR) [Note: There is no requirement to keep copies of CMIRs.]

    c) TD F 90–22.1-Report of Foreign Bank and Financial Accounts (FBAR)

    d) Form 109-Suspicious Activity Report by Money Services Business (SAR-MSB)

4. Copy of the Form 107-Registration of Money Services Business (MSB Registration) and acknowledgement letter provided by the Detroit Computing Center.

5. If you are an agent, copies of all contracts or trust agreements as they relate to your capacity as an agent.

6. If you are an agent of a money transmitter please contact the main office and request a CD-Rom that includes all of the funds transmittals $____ and greater for the following time period: _____

Please send a copy of the AML program at least two weeks before the appointment date.

Information Due By		At Next Appointment		Mail In	
	Name and Title of Requestor				Date:
FROM	Office Location:		Phone:		Page 120
			Fax:		

APPENDIX E – FINCEN SAR QUALITY GUIDANCE

Suggestions for Addressing Common Errors Noted in Suspicious Activity Reporting

The Financial Crimes Enforcement Network ("FinCEN") has noticed common errors in the filing of Suspicious Activity Reports ("SARs").[89]   Although these errors were noted primarily through studying Suspicious Activity Reports by MSB (Form 109) filings, we believe that publishing an explanation of ten of the most common errors and ways much of them readily can be mitigated could be informative to financial institutions in other industries in their efforts to implement simple strategies to provide accurate and complete information in their SAR filings. We also expect that SAR filers who are trained on the requirements would already have available the information necessary to complete the SAR properly, meaning that significant improvements to the SAR filing could be made without significant additional efforts beyond those already undertaken for the investigation and decision to file a SAR which may contain errors.

It is critical that the information provided in a SAR filing be as accurate and complete as possible. SAR information provides a valuable tool to FinCEN, law enforcement, regulatory authorities, and intelligence agencies (collectively referred to as "users"), allowing the observation of larger patterns of suspicious activity, which might not have otherwise been detected. When combined with other sources, the information generated from SAR filings also plays an important role for law enforcement agencies in identifying potentially illegal activities, such as money laundering and terrorist financing, and assists in detecting and preventing the flow of illicit funds through our financial system.

We have identified three areas where financial institutions should concentrate efforts to ensure information contained in the SAR is complete: (1) SAR narratives, (2) certain critical fields that allow users to analyze quickly where activity has occurred, and (3) fields that identify the type, category and character of the suspicious activity.

(1) The Importance of Complete SAR Narratives

In general, an accurate and complete SAR narrative should identify the five essential elements - *who? what? when? where? and why?* - of the suspicious activity being reported. SAR narratives should describe, as fully as possible, why the activity or transaction is unusual for the customer, taking into consideration the types of products and services offered by your industry and the nature and typical activities of similar

---

89. Issued October 10, 2007. Also available at
      http://www.fincen.gov/SAR_Common_Errors_Web_Posting.pdf.

customers. Explaining why the transaction is suspicious is critical. The following are common responses received in the SAR narrative field which do **not** allow users to fully utilize the information submitted.

Empty Narrative Field: The narrative field in the form must explain **why** the transaction was suspicious. If the narrative field is left blank, the information in the SAR only addresses the "who/what/when/where" of the transaction. Each SAR filing must have a narrative that accurately explains the nature and circumstances of the suspicious activity. Otherwise, the information contained in the SAR is of limited utility.

Failure to Explain Information in Supporting Documents: All SAR Form Instructions specifically state that the attachment of supporting documentation is prohibited. Supporting documents cannot be uploaded into the database and should not be used as a substitute for the narrative, since law enforcement, FinCEN and other intelligence agencies cannot readily view the documents or the information contained therein. The information appearing in any such supporting documentation should be reasonably described in the narrative and must be maintained for five years to be made available upon specific request.

Inadequate Narratives: Any narrative that does not accurately and completely explain the nature and circumstances of the suspicious activity is an inadequate narrative. In general, most inadequate narratives merely repeat data in the form's fixed fields (for example, "John Doe sent two money transfers on 1/1/2007.", or "Wired $2,000 to Mexico."). Restating the information found in critical fields does not sufficiently illustrate *why* the transaction was suspicious, considering the nature and expected activities of the institution's customers.

(2) Responses in Fields of Critical Value

The responses provided in fields of critical value, marked by an asterisk (*) in most SAR forms, are examined by users to track activity and follow-up on leads provided in SARs. This information is also used by FinCEN to develop analytical products that are distributed to law enforcement, regulators and other intelligence agencies, as well as to provide general feedback to financial institutions . The quality of this information is of utmost importance; when inaccurate or incomplete information is provided, its utility is diminished significantly. Several common issues arising from reports including inaccurate or incomplete information in critical fields are listed immediately below.

Inaccurate Special Responses: As noted in the instructions to the SAR forms, specific responses are required when data is unavailable. Institutions should not create their own responses. Special responses (for example, "N/A" or "Same as above") pose as real data and distort statistics on how often certain items of data are unavailable. It is extremely important that reporting institutions follow the instructions on the form and input the proper responses for unavailable information.

Missing or Incomplete Filer Employer Identification Number ("EIN"): The EIN of the reporting institution permits regulators and law enforcement to follow transactions properly through entities that report them. A reporting institution is expected to know its EIN and report it accurately. Invalid or incomplete entries are unacceptable. EIN entries of "000000000" and "999999999" are examples of invalid entries. Incomplete EINs have fewer than nine digits and are usually the result of the preparer entering the EIN with a hyphen in a nine-digit fill-in field, causing the last digit of the number to disappear. Incomplete entries are also created by typographical errors that were not caught in review.

Missing Filer Telephone Number: SAR information users must have the ability to contact the reporting financial institution to follow up on any leads relating to possible criminal activity. The telephone numbers of the financial institution, including the specific transaction location, are critical for this reason, and must be included in any SAR filing. To reiterate, hyphens should not be included in the critical fields.

Invalid Subject Social Security Number ("SSN")/EIN: The SAR forms and the E-filing manual provide specific instructions regarding acceptable entries in the SSN/EIN fields when the respective number is unknown. Consult the form instructions or the E-filing instructions when completing these sections. Entries of "000000000" and "999999999" are examples of invalid entries that cause an inaccurate record of the activity, which is of no value to those who utilize SAR information.

Incomplete Subject Information; Government Issued Identification: The method used to identify the subject should be as complete as possible. A driver's license or passport provides law enforcement with the information necessary to find out *who* a subject is and *where* a subject may be located. The exclusion of an identification number when the issuer is known is an example of a commonly received incomplete response. If a government issued identification card or document was used during the transaction, then both the number and issuer of the identification card or document should be provided.

(3) Identifying the Category and Character of Suspicious Activity

By filling out SARs as accurately and completely as possible, financial institutions help mitigate their risk by maintaining a strong component of their anti-money laundering ("AML") programs. Employee training in the recognition of suspicious activity and the proper filing of SARs protects the financial institution and aids law enforcement in apprehending criminals. Possible characterizations of suspicious activity and their descriptions can be found in SAR Activity Review Issue 7. The following are common responses received in the SAR fields which identify the type of suspicious activity. The lack of accurate and complete information addressed below hinders the usage of SAR information.

Missing Category, Type, or Characterization of Suspicious Activity: It is important for users to know why the activity is being reported and how the activity may relate to ongoing investigations. The category, type, or characterization of suspicious activity is important in this regard. This field should never be blank. If none of the available options appear to apply to the particular activity that is being reported, then the "other" box should be checked, and a brief and informative description should be entered in the "other" text field, if provided, or in the narrative.

Incorrect Characterization of Suspicious Activity: In order to provide accurate information to all users, FinCEN reviews narratives and other SAR data to verify that the category of suspicious activity appears correct. Many times, the characterization of suspicious activity appears incorrect or has not been selected. In these cases, there is no information in the SAR to substantiate the checked selections. For example, an institution may report that a customer comes in frequently to purchase monetary instruments below the $3,000 recordkeeping threshold, indicating the potential that the customer could be "structuring" transactions; however, the narrative does not provide any information about previous transactions, and there are no prior SARs filed on the subject of the SAR.

Conclusion

When accurate and complete, SARs are an important tool in combating financial crimes. When completed correctly, the forms provide its users with important information that can be used to analyze broad sets of data and to apprehend suspected criminals and terrorists. When the SAR forms are filled out incorrectly or are incomplete, they generally do not provide useful and adequate information, and in some cases, distort information reviewed by FinCEN and other users. Further, by filling out SARs as accurately and completely as possible, financial institutions also maintain a picture of the identified, suspicious transactions flowing through them, which may be of use in their BSA/AML Program for risk mitigation purposes.

In our continuing effort to make BSA compliance more efficient and effective, we are providing below some simple suggestions that may reduce incomplete and/or incorrect SARs. As BSA/AML Programs are designed on a risk-basis by financial institutions to meet their own specific needs, some of the following suggestions may not be directly applicable.

1. *Sign up for BSA E-filing.* This will eliminate errors of omission because preparers must enter the required data or a special response in critical fields. Information on signing up for E-filing can be found on www.fincen.gov by clicking on "BSA E-filing" or by calling 1-888-827-2778 (option 6).

2. *Provide staff and preparers with training on recognizing suspicious activity and avoiding SAR filing errors.* This training will help the financial institution maintain an effective AML compliance program, as well as protect the institution from potential abuse by criminals.

3. *Provide preparers with examples of accurate and complete SAR filings with "John Doe" data in the fields.* This will allow preparers to see the correct format of a completed SAR form and can serve as a reference point for future filings. Please ensure that these sample or mock forms are not filed with FinCEN.

4. *Ensure that preparers know the company EIN, address, telephone number, contact office, etc., for the Reporting Business and Contact for Assistance fields.* This will allow the preparers to provide FinCEN with accurate reporting information, as well as provide law enforcement with accurate contact information should further investigation be required.

5. *Provide preparers with the instructions for completing the form currently in use.* When a new form is released, do not rely on old instructions and training because there likely will be significant changes. While form changes are infrequent, being up-to-date on the most current forms helps financial institutions with their regulatory compliance requirements and enables them to provide FinCEN and other users with the most accurate data possible.

6. *Provide preparers with the FinCEN Regulatory Helpline number, (800) 949-2732, the FinCEN homepage, www.fincen.gov, and the MSB homepage, www.MSB.gov.*

7. *Have a second reviewer to ensure accuracy and completeness.* An additional review of the SAR will help to eliminate errors and omissions.

APPENDIX F – SAR SUPPORTING DOCUMENTATION GUIDANCE

FinCEN Guidance on Suspicious Activity Report Supporting Documentation[90]

The Financial Crimes Enforcement Network (FinCEN)[91] is issuing this guidance to clarify:

(1) The Bank Secrecy Act (BSA) requirement that financial institutions provide Suspicious Activity Report (SAR) supporting documentation in response to requests by FinCEN and appropriate law enforcement or supervisory agencies;[92]

(2) What constitutes "supporting documentation" under SAR regulations;[93] and

(3) When legal process is required for disclosure of supporting documentation.

(1) Disclosure of Supporting Documentation to FinCEN and Appropriate Law Enforcement or Supervisory Agencies

When a financial institution files a SAR, it is required to maintain a copy of the SAR and the original or business record equivalent of any supporting documentation for a period of five years from the date of filing the SAR.[94] Financial institutions must provide all documentation supporting the filing of a SAR upon request by FinCEN or an appropriate law enforcement[95] or supervisory agency.[96]

---

90. FIN-2007-G003 (issued June 13, 2007). Also available at http://www.fincen.gov/statutes_regs/guidance/pdf/Supporting_Documentation_Guidance.pdf.

91. FinCEN consulted with staffs of the Department of Justice, the Federal Bureau of Investigation, the Internal Revenue Service's Criminal Investigation Division, the United States Secret Service, the Department of Homeland Security's Immigration and Customs Enforcement, the Drug Enforcement Administration, the Board of Governors of the Federal Reserve System, the Office of the Comptroller of the Currency, the Federal Deposit Insurance Corporation, the Office of Thrift Supervision, the National Credit Union Administration, the Commodity Futures Trading Commission, and the Securities and Exchange Commission prior to issuing this guidance.

92. See 31 CFR § 103.15(c); 31 CFR § 103.16(e); 31 CFR § 103.17(d); 31 CFR § 103.18(d); 31 CFR § 103.19(d); 31 CFR § 103.20(c); and 31 CFR § 103.21(d)

93. Id.

94. Id.

95. See *"Providing Suspicious Activity Reports to Appropriate Law Enforcement,"* SAR Activity Review: Trends, Tips & Issues, Issue 9 (Oct. 2005), p.43, http://www.fincen.gov/sarreviewissue9.pdf.

96. Supervisory agencies have independent statutory authority to examine all books and records of the financial institutions for which they are the appropriate regulator.

When requested to provide supporting documentation, financial institutions should take special care to verify that a requestor of information is, in fact, a representative of FinCEN or an appropriate law enforcement or supervisory agency. A financial institution should incorporate procedures for such verification into its BSA compliance or anti-money laundering program. These procedures may include, for example, independent employment verification with the requestor's field office or face-to-face review of the requestor's credentials.

Disclosure of SARs to appropriate law enforcement and supervisory agencies is protected by the safe harbor provisions applicable to both voluntary and mandatory suspicious activity reporting by financial institutions.[97]

(2) What Constitutes Supporting Documentation

"Supporting documentation" refers to all documents or records that assisted a financial institution in making the determination that certain activity required a SAR filing. A financial institution must identify supporting documentation at the time the SAR is filed,[98] and this documentation must be maintained by the institution as such. The manner in which a financial institution maintains supporting documentation may vary from institution to institution, but each institution should prescribe its own method in its anti-money laundering program written procedures. For instance, a financial institution's procedures may require that all supporting documentation for a particular SAR be segregated in a single file folder or scanned and maintained in a data file.

What qualifies as supporting documentation depends on the facts and circumstances of each filing. As indicated in each of the SAR forms, financial institutions should identify in the SAR narrative the supporting documentation, which may include, for example, transaction records, new account information, tape recordings, e-mail messages, and correspondence. While items identified in the narrative of the SAR generally constitute supporting documentation, a document or record may qualify as supporting documentation even if not identified in the narrative.

---

97. The BSA provides protection from civil liability for all reports of suspicious transactions made to appropriate authorities, including supporting documentation, regardless of whether such reports are mandatory. Specifically, the BSA provides that a financial institution, or a director, officer, employee, or agent of a financial institution, that makes a "voluntary disclosure of any possible violation of law or regulation to a government agency" shall not be liable to any person under "any law or regulation of the United States, any constitution, law, or regulation of any State or political subdivision of any State, or under any contract or other legally enforceable agreement (including any arbitration agreement), for such disclosure or for any failure to provide notice of such disclosure to the person who is the subject of such disclosure or any other person identified in the disclosure." 31 U.S.C. § 5318(g)(3).

98. Suspicious Transactions Reporting Requirements, 61 Fed. Reg. 4326, 4330 (February 5, 1996). Supporting documentation should **not** be attached to the SAR filing.

---

(3) No Legal Process is Required for Disclosure of Supporting Documentation

The Right to Financial Privacy Act (RFPA) generally prohibits financial institutions from disclosing a customer's financial records to a Government agency without service of legal process, notice to the customer and an opportunity to challenge the disclosure.[99] However, no such requirement applies when the financial institution provides the financial records or information to FinCEN or a supervisory agency in the exercise of its "supervisory, regulatory or monetary functions."[100] In addition, no such requirement applies when FinCEN or an appropriate law enforcement or supervisory agency requests either a copy of a SAR or supporting documentation underlying the SAR.

With respect to supporting documentation, rules under the BSA state explicitly that financial institutions must retain copies of supporting documentation, that supporting documentation is "deemed to have been filed with" the SAR, and that financial institutions must provide supporting documentation upon request.[101] FinCEN has interpreted these regulations under the BSA as requiring a financial institution to provide supporting documentation even in the absence of legal process. FinCEN understands that this is in accord with the RFPA, which states that nothing in the act "authorize(s) the withholding of financial records or information required to be reported in accordance with any Federal statute or rule promulgated thereunder."[102]

---

99. This guidance is only applicable to financial records or information that constitute supporting documentation pursuant to provisions in the Bank Secrecy Act that govern the reporting of suspicious transactions. Consequently, nothing in this guidance is intended to alter or modify the duties or obligations of financial institutions subject to the Right to Financial Privacy Act (12 U.S.C. § 3401, et seq.), 18 U.S.C. § 1510, or similar provisions of law. When responding to law enforcement requests for customer financial records or information other than SAR supporting documentation, financial institutions subject to the RFPA must still comply with that statute's notice and challenge provisions in the absence of an applicable exception, e.g., service of a grand jury subpoena or a national security letter.

100. See 12 U.S.C. § 3413(b).

101. See 31 CFR § 103.15(c); 31 CFR § 103.16(e); 31 CFR § 103.17(d); 31 CFR § 103.18(d); 31 CFR § 103.19(d); 31 CFR § 103.20(c); and 31 CFR § 103.21(d).

102. See 12 U.S.C. 3413(d).

APPENDIX G – SAMPLE MSB INTERVIEW QUESTIONS

This sample provides a list of initial interview questions that an examiner may consider using during interviews while on examination. Examiners should ask follow up questions based on the responses to initial questions. This sample is not inclusive. The actual questions asked will depend on the type of financial services provided by the MSB. Questions may also vary by agency performing the examination.

Date

Location of Interview_____

Name of Entity_____

Address_____

City and State_____

Telephone Number_____

Business ID#_____

Owner(s)_____

Manager(s) _____

Name of Person Interviewed and Job Title_____

Sample Background Questions Applicable to All Types of MSBs

1. Please describe your business experience (financial services, other work history).

2. When did you start providing monetary services?

3. Where did the funds come from to start the MSB? (Initial investment, partners, other owners, etc.)

4. Was the business purchased from another owner or was it started from the "ground up?"

5. Do you or your partners have other businesses or business interests? Have you or your partners purchased, or do you have ownership interests in other MSBs? (Get names and addresses.)

6. How long has the business been at its current location?

7. Legal form of business – Corporation/Partnership/Sole Proprietor

8. What are the names of the owners/principal shareholders? What are the names/titles of the corporate officers?

9. How often do shareholders/owners meet? Are minutes taken of these meetings? Review minutes for BSA compliance issues.

10. Has the business had a prior BSA examination? If yes, get copy of report of examination.

11. Do you belong to any industry trade groups or associations?

12. Are you an agent of another MSB? If yes:

    a. What is the name of your principal(s)?

    b. What BSA guidance do you receive from your principal?

    c. What contracts or agreements did you sign to become an agent?

    d. Did you receive BSA training from your principal?

13. Are you a headquarters, regional, or branch operation? Get names, addresses, phone numbers of all MSBs in the group.

14. If the MSB under examination is the MSB headquarters, how many agents does the MSB have? Obtain a copy of agent list.

15. What days of the week is the business open? Hours open?

16. What types of financial services do you provide?

_____ Check cashing	_____ Money transmission
_____ Traveler's checks	_____ Money orders
_____ Currency exchanges	_____ Stored value cards
_____ Telephone cards	_____ E-bill payments
_____ Other (list)	

17. What other types of businesses are conducted at your location? (Grocery sale, gasoline sales, liquor sales, jeweler, etc.)

18. Do you provide other financial services to your customers? (Insurance, tax preparation etc.?)

19. How many employees do you have at each location? How are they paid?

20. What BSA training do you provide to its employees? Do you keep training logs? Do you have a training manual?

21. What U.S. banks do you use? (Get bank name, account number, signatory authority, etc.)

22. What are your banking procedures for the cash received from the monetary services that you provide? Do you use special accounts for your MSB transactions?

23. Who makes the bank deposits?

24. How do you know that employees have accounted for all cash and that the funds are either deposited into the bank or kept in the safe? Describe internal control procedures and policies.

25. How much currency do you start the day with?

___ U.S. dollars?

___ Type and value of foreign currency?

26. What customers do you target? How do you advertise to reach those customers?

27. Who are your regular customers?

28. What ID is required to conduct a MSB transaction? What ID records are kept and how are those records maintained? (Digital, scanned, paper copy)

___ How do you ensure that all the required ID records are complete?

___ What are your policies and procedures to verify the ID of a customer?

29. Do you temporarily hold funds for customers that are not recorded in the records?

30. Do you make payments on behalf of your customers?

31. Do you provide services to or have transactions with other MSBs such as check cashing, transportation of currency, or sales of money orders/traveler's checks?

32. Have you ever loaned another MSB currency or other funds?

33. Have you ever used another MSB's bank account?

34. Do you have a risk assessment of your business? Is your AML program based upon this risk assessment? If not, what is the basis of your AML program?

35. What types of records do you maintain? (Customer identification number, source documents such as invoices, receipts, etc.)

36. How long do you retain these records?

37. How do you store these records? (Paper copy, electronically, digitally, etc.)

38. What systems do you have in place to determine if a transaction that meets BSA filing requirements is detected?

    ___ Please describe your process for reporting currency transactions, including how you detect "multiple transactions", i.e., transactions conduct by one customer who uses multiple MSB services.

    ___ Walk through the transaction process.

39. Please describe your process for reporting currency transactions.

40. How do you monitor the day-to-day activities of your business?

41. What are your policies and procedures to prevent a customer from making transactions on behalf of a person unknown to you or for other customers?

42. What procedures do you have in place to detect suspicious activities? Note: Check cashers are not required to file SAR-MSBs.

43. What are your procedures for reporting suspicious activities?

44. Do you have records or documentation to support your decisions when not filing a SAR-MSB?

45. Do you file and retain a copy of the MSB registration (if applicable), CTRs, FBARs, CMIRS, and SAR-MSBs?

46. Multiple branches, agents, or locations – How do you decide who should file BSA reports? Are the policies and procedures written?

47. Who files or makes the decision not to file BSA reports?

48. Do you have an internal audit department? Have you had an independent BSA/AML review?

49. Do you have international affiliates/business partners?

50. Do you have any international business?

51. Do you physically transport currency or monetary instruments into or out of the United States? If yes:

    ___ How is the currency transported? (Get details such as how, vehicles used, etc.)

    ___ Who are the customers for which you provide this service?

    ___ What are your fees for this service?

    ___ How do you record these transactions?

    ___ Have you filed CMIR reports?

52. Do you mail to or receive currency or monetary instruments from sources outside the United States? If yes:

   ___ Who are the customers for which you provide this service?

   ___ What are your fees for this service?

   ___ How do you record these transactions?

   ___Have you filed CMIR reports?

53. Do you have an interest or signatory authority in any foreign financial account? (If yes, get name and address of financial institution where the account is maintained, account number, signatory authority, etc.)

54. Who does the daily bookkeeping? What services does your accountant provide for you?

Additional Questions – Comments

Sample Currency Dealer or Exchanger Questions

1. What types of transactions do you conduct as a currency dealer or exchanger?

2. How much foreign currency do you keep on hand? (Get daily inventory sheet.)

3. Where do you get the foreign currency?

4. How do record your exchanges? (Over the counter and vault.) Who records the daily log? Are records computerized? (Follow a transaction through the records.)

5. How do you determine your profit on an exchange? Do you ever do any exchanges without a profit?

6. Who conducts the "retail" or "over the counter" transactions?
   Name:
   Identification:

7. Who conducts the "vault" transactions?
   Name:
   Identification:

8. Where do you have your safes?

Sample Check Casher Questions

1. Do you have monetary limits for cashing checks? Does the limit change depending on the type of check? (Government, payroll, personal, third-party)

2. What type of accounting system do you use to record transactions? (Double entry, computerized, general ledger, journals, etc.)

3. How do you handle a check of over $10,000? (Approval process, customer ID, cash controls, etc.)

4. Where do you get the cash/currency to cash checks?

5. How do you ensure that employees have not taken cash from the business? Describe procedures, records maintained, persons responsible for cash transactions and internal controls of cash and BSA monitoring/reporting.

6. Do you use "customer cards" (records that have customer ID and check cashing history)?

7. Do you have daily summary cash reconciliation or other records that reconcile the daily cash on hand, sources, uses to ending cash on hand?

8. What is your approval procedure for check cashing?

9. Do you cash checks for customers who do not have ID?

10. Do you cash third party business checks? If so, what procedures in place to monitor the BSA reporting requirements? Do you hold cash for these customers?

11. Do you display your check cashing fee structure? Are there different fees for different types of customers?

12. Do you deposit all the cashed checks from the day's sales into the bank on the same day? (Does the MSB mix one day's sales with another? For example, combine afternoon from day 1 with morning checks cashed from day 2.)

13. Do you have insurance for your cash inventory? What is the maximum limit?

Sample Money Transmitter Questions

1. How do you know that you have accounted for all your funds transmittals over the course of a given day? (For example, employees are not sending money without receiving payment for the funds transmittal.) Describe internal control policies and procedures.

2. How do you handle a funds transmittal of over $10,000? (Approval process, customer ID, cash controls, etc.)

3. Do you accept cash or credit card payments for funds transmittals?

4. Who prepares the funds transmittal forms? Do you have special forms for international funds transmittals? Who signs the forms?

5. Who completes the funds transmission when a customer is receiving money?

6. How much cash is available on a daily basis to cover funds transmittal payouts?

Sample Questions for Issuance or Sale of Money Orders/Traveler's Checks

1. What is the name of the money order/traveler's check service you provide?

2. Are there limits on the dollar value of money orders/traveler's checks? How are the limits set?

3. Would you accept more than $10,000 in currency for money orders/traveler's checks? How do you account (books and records) for this type of transaction?

4. Do you accept checks or credit card purchases for money orders/traveler's checks?

5. Do you cash money orders/traveler's checks? What ID do you require?

6. Do you have a special form for traveler's checks that are to be sent outside the United States?

APPENDIX H– GUIDANCE FOR MSBS WITH FOREIGN COUNTERPARTIES OR AGENTS

FinCEN Interpretive Release 2004-1 - Anti-Money Laundering Program Requirements for Money Services Businesses With Respect to Foreign Agents or Foreign Counterparties

This Interpretive Guidance sets forth our interpretation of the regulation requiring Money Services Businesses that are required to register with FinCEN to establish and maintain anti-money laundering programs.[103] See 31 CFR 103.125. Specifically, this Interpretive Guidance clarifies that the anti-money laundering program regulation requires Money Services Businesses to establish adequate and appropriate policies, procedures, and controls commensurate with the risks of money laundering and the financing of terrorism posed by their relationship with foreign agents or foreign counterparties of the Money Services Business.[104]

Under existing Bank Secrecy Act regulations, we have defined Money Services Businesses to include five distinct types of financial services providers and the U.S. Postal Service: (1) Currency dealers or exchangers; (2) check cashers; (3) issuers of traveler's checks, money orders, or stored value cards (4) sellers or redeemers of traveler's checks, money orders, or stored value; and (5) money transmitters. See 31 CFR 103.11(uu). With limited exception, Money Services Businesses are subject to the

---

103. See FinCEN Release Number 2004-1, Anti-Money Laundering Requirements for Money Services Businesses with Respect to Foreign Agents or Foreign Counterparties, 69 Federal Register 74439, December 14, 2004.

104. This Interpretive Guidance focuses on the need to control risks arising out of the relationship between a Money Services Business and its foreign counterparty or agent. Under existing FinCEN regulations, only Money Services Business principals are required to register with FinCEN, and only Money Services Business principals establish the counterparty or agency relationships. 31 CFR 103.41. Accordingly this Interpretive Guidance only applies to those Money Services Businesses required to register with FinCEN, that is, only those Money Services Businesses that may have a relationship with a foreign agent or counterparty.

full range of Bank Secrecy Act regulatory controls, including the anti-money laundering program rule, suspicious activity and currency transaction reporting rules, and various other identification and recordkeeping rules.[105]

Many Money Services Businesses, including the vast majority of money transmitters in the United States, operate through a system of agents both domestically and internationally. We estimate that a substantial majority of all cross-border remittances by money transmitters are conducted using this model. Other Money Services Businesses may operate through more informal relationships, such as the trust-based hawala system.[106] Regardless of the form of the relationship between a Money Services Business and its foreign agents or counterparties, Money Services Business transactions generally are initiated by customers seeking to send or receive funds, cash checks, buy or sell money orders or traveler's checks, or buy or sell currency. The customer directs the Money Services Business to execute the transactions; the Money Services Business does not unilaterally determine the recipient of its products or services. Although the customer can use the Money Services Business' services, the customer does not typically establish an account relationship with the Money Services Business. The focus of this Interpretive Guidance is the establishment of, and ongoing relationship between, a Money Services Business and its foreign agent or foreign counterparty that facilitates the flow of funds cross-border into and out of the United States on behalf of customers.

The Cross-Border Flow of Funds through Money Services Businesses and Associated Risks

Ensuring that financial institutions based in the United States establish and apply adequate and appropriate policies, procedures, and controls in their anti-money laundering compliance programs to protect the international gateways to the U.S. financial system is an essential element of the Bank Secrecy Act regulatory regime. This Interpretive Guidance forms a part of our comprehensive approach to accomplishing this goal. To the extent Money Services Businesses utilize relationships with foreign agents or counterparties to facilitate the movement of funds into or out of the United States, they must take reasonable steps to guard against the flow of illicit funds, or the flow of funds

---

105. See 31 CFR 103.125 (requirement for Money Services Businesses to establish and maintain an anti-money laundering compliance program); 31 CFR 103.22 (requirement for Money Services Businesses to file currency transaction reports); 31 CFR 103.20 (requirement for Money Services Businesses, other than check cashers and issuers, sellers, or redeemers of stored value, to file suspicious activity reports); 31 CFR 103.29 (requirement for Money Services Businesses that sell money orders, traveler's checks, or other instruments for cash to verify the identity of the customer and create and maintain a record of each cash purchase between $3,000 and $10,000, inclusive); 31 CFR 103.33(f) (requirement for Money Services Businesses that send or accept instructions to transmit funds of $3,000 or more to verify the identity of the sender or receiver and create and maintain a record of the transmittal regardless of the method of payment); and 31 CFR 103.37 (requirement for currency exchangers to create and maintain a record of each exchange of currency in excess of $1,000).

106. For an analysis of informal value transfer systems, see FinCEN's Report to Congress Pursuant to Section 359 of the PATRIOT Act, available on www.fincen.gov.

from legitimate sources to persons seeking to use those funds for illicit purposes, through such relationships. The money laundering or terrorism financing risks associated with foreign agents or counterparties are similar to the risks presented by domestic agents of Money Services Businesses. For example, the foreign agent of the domestic Money Services Business may have lax anti-money laundering policies, procedures, and internal controls, or actually may be complicit with those seeking to move illicit funds. In some instances, the risk with foreign agents can be greater than with domestic agents because foreign agents are not subject to the Bank Secrecy Act regulatory regime; the extent to which they are subject to anti-money laundering regulation, and the quality of that regulation, will vary with the jurisdictions in which they are located.

There are a variety of ways in which a Money Services Business may be susceptible to the unwitting facilitation of money laundering through foreign agents or counterparties. For example, our review of Bank Secrecy Act data revealed several instances of suspected criminal activity— detected by existing anti-money laundering and suspicious activity reporting programs of Money Services Businesses and banks— where foreign agents of Money Services Business have engaged in bulk sales of sequentially numbered, U.S. denominated traveler's checks or blocks of money orders, to one or two individuals. The individuals involved frequently purchased the instruments on multiple dates and in different locations, structuring the purchases to avoid reporting thresholds and issuer limits on daily instrument sales. The instruments usually had illegible signatures or failed to designate a beneficiary or payor. The instruments were then negotiated with one or more dealers in goods, such as diamonds, gems, or precious metals, deposited in foreign banks, and cleared through U.S. banks. In such cases, the clearing banks were so far removed from the transactions that they could not trace back or screen either the intervening transactions or the individuals involved in the transactions.

A case involving suspicious activity in a Money Services Business' domestic agent provides a further example of the type of high-risk activity that also may be engaged in by foreign agents or counterparties. In this instance, the domestic Money Services Business had policies, procedures, and controls that facilitated the detection of illicit activity at the agent. A group of six customers entered a money transmitter agent at approximately five-minute intervals to send the same structured amounts ($2,500) to the same receiver in a foreign country. Several weeks later, another group of six customers entered the same agent location and conducted an identical pattern of successive $2,500 transfers (a few minutes apart) to the same recipient in the same foreign country as the first set of transactions. Some of the individuals in the second group had the same last names as customers in the first group. Additional suspicious activity reports filed by the primary Money Services Business identified several other groups of customers initiating money transfers at this same agent business location, in the same manner, and in the same overall time frame. This activity by an agent drew the scrutiny of the Money Services Business, and in addition to the filing of suspicious activity reports, led to the termination of the relationship of the Money Services Business with the agent. These examples of illicit activity occurring at the agents of Money Services Businesses underscore the need for Money Services Businesses to include, as a part of their anti-money laundering programs, procedures, policies, and controls to govern relationships with foreign agents and counterparties to enable the Money Services Business to perform the appropriate level of suspicious activity and risk monitoring. We believe that this obligation is an essential part of each Money Services Business' existing obligation under 31 CFR 103.125 to develop and implement an effective anti-money laundering program.[107]

This Interpretive Guidance will aid Money Services Businesses in adopting appropriate risk-based policies, procedures, and controls on cross-border relationships with foreign agents and counterparties.

Anti-Money Laundering Program Elements Relating to Foreign Agents and Counterparties

Under 31 CFR 103.125(a), Money Services Businesses are required to develop, implement, and maintain an effective anti-money laundering program reasonably designed to prevent the Money Services Business from being used to facilitate money laundering and the financing of terrorist activities. The program must be commensurate with the risks posed by the location, size, nature, and volume of the financial services provided by the Money Services Business. Additionally, the program must incorporate policies, procedures, and controls reasonably designed to assure compliance with the Bank Secrecy Act and implementing regulations.

With respect to Money Services Businesses that utilize foreign agents or counterparties, a Money Services Business' anti-money laundering program must include risk-based policies, procedures, and controls designed to identify and minimize money laundering and terrorist financing risks associated with foreign agents and counterparties that facilitate the flow of funds into and out of the United States. The program must be aimed at preventing the products and services of the Money Services Business from being used to facilitate money laundering or terrorist financing through these relationships and detecting the use of these products and services for money laundering or terrorist financing by the Money Services Business or agent. Relevant risk factors may include, but are not limited to:

- The foreign agent or counterparty's location and jurisdiction of organization, chartering, or licensing. This would include considering the extent to which the relevant jurisdiction is internationally recognized as presenting a greater risk for money laundering or is considered to have more robust anti-money laundering standards.

---

107. FinCEN previously interpreted 31 CFR 103.125 to impose a similar obligation on a money transmitter with respect to its domestic agents. See Matter of Western Union, No. 2003–2 (Mar. 6, 2003) (www.fincen.gov).

- The ownership of the foreign agent or counterparty. This includes whether the owners are known, upon reasonable inquiry, to be associated with criminal conduct or terrorism. For example, have the individuals been designated by Treasury's Office of Foreign Assets Control as Specially Designated Nationals or Blocked Persons (e.g., involvement in terrorism, drug trafficking, or the proliferation of weapons of mass destruction)

- The extent to which the foreign agent or counterparty is subject to anti-money laundering requirements in its jurisdiction and whether it has established such controls.

- Any information known or readily available to the Money Services Business about the foreign agent or counterparty's anti-money laundering record, including public information in industry guides, periodicals, and major publications.

- The nature of the foreign agent or counterparty's business, the markets it serves, and the extent to which its business and the markets it serves present an increased risk for money laundering or terrorist financing.

- The types and purpose of services to be provided to, and anticipated activity with, the foreign agent or counterparty.

- The nature and duration of the Money Services Business' relationship with the foreign agent or counterparty.

Specifically, a Money Services Business' anti-money laundering program should include procedures for the following:

1. Conduct of Due Diligence on Foreign Agents and Counterparties

Money Services Businesses should establish procedures for conducting reasonable, risk-based due diligence on potential and existing foreign agents and counterparties to help ensure that such foreign agents and counterparties are not themselves complicit in illegal activity involving the Money Services Business' products and services, and that they have in place appropriate anti-money laundering controls to guard against the abuse of the Money Services Business' products and services. Such due diligence must, at a minimum, include reasonable procedures to identify the owners of the Money Services Business' foreign agents and counterparties, as well as to evaluate, on an ongoing basis, the operations of those foreign agents and counterparties and their implementation of policies, procedures, and controls reasonably designed to help assure that the Money Services Business' products and services are not subject to abuse by the foreign agent's or counterparty's customers, employees, or contractors.[108]

---

108. Our anti-money laundering program rule 31 CFR 103.125(d)(iii) permits Money Services Businesses to satisfy this last requirement with regard to their domestic agents (which are also Money Services Businesses under BSA regulations) by allocating responsibility for the program to their agents. Such an allocation, however, does not relieve a Money Services Business from ultimate responsibility for establishing and maintaining an effective anti-money laundering program. *Id.*

2. Risk-based Monitoring of Foreign Agents or Counterparties

In addition to the due diligence described above, in order to detect and report suspected money laundering or terrorist financing, Money Services Businesses should establish procedures for risk-based monitoring and review of transactions from, to, or through the United States that are conducted through foreign agents and counterparties.[109] Such procedures should also focus on identifying material changes in the agent's risk profile, such as a change in ownership, business, or the regulatory scrutiny to which it is subject.

The review of transactions should enable the Money Services Business to identify and, where appropriate, report as suspicious such occurrences as: instances of unusual wire activity, bulk sales or purchases of sequentially numbered instruments, multiple purchases or sales that appear to be structured, and illegible or missing customer information. Additionally, Money Services Businesses should establish procedures to assure that their foreign agents or counterparties are effectively implementing an anti-money laundering program and to discern obvious breakdowns in the implementation of the program by the foreign agent or counterparty.

Similarly, money transmitters should have procedures in place to enable them to review foreign agent or counterparty activity for signs of structuring or unnecessarily complex transmissions through multiple jurisdictions that may be indicative of layering. Such procedures should also enable them to discern attempts to evade identification or other requirements, whether imposed by applicable law or by the Money Services Business' own internal policies. Activity by agents or counterparties that appears aimed at evading the Money Services Business' own controls can be indicative of complicity in illicit conduct; this activity must be scrutinized, reported as appropriate, and corrective action taken as warranted.

3. Corrective Action and Termination

Money Services Businesses should have procedures for responding to foreign agents or counterparties that present unreasonable risks of money laundering or the financing of terrorism. Such procedures should provide for the implementation of corrective action on the part of the foreign agent or counterparty or for the termination of the relationship with any foreign agent or counterparty that the Money Services Business determines poses an unacceptable risk of money laundering or terrorist financing, or that has demonstrated systemic, willful, or repeated lapses in compliance with the Money Services Business' own anti-money laundering procedures or requirements.

---

109. Nothing in this Interpretive Guidance is intended to require Money Services Businesses to monitor or review, for purposes of the Bank Secrecy Act, transactions or activities of foreign agents or counterparties that occur entirely outside of the United States and do not flow from, to, or through the United States.

While Money Services Businesses may already have implemented some or all of the procedures described in this Interpretive Guidance as a part of their anti-money laundering programs, we wish to provide a reasonable period of time for all affected Money Services Businesses to assess their operations, review their existing policies and programs for compliance with this Advisory, and implement any additional necessary changes. We will expect full compliance with this Interpretive Release within 180 days.

Finally, we are mindful of the potential impact that this Interpretive Release may have on continuing efforts to bring informal value transfer systems into compliance with the existing regulatory framework of the Bank Secrecy Act. Experience has demonstrated the challenges in securing compliance by, for instance, hawalas and other informal value transfer systems. Further specification of Bank Secrecy Act compliance obligations carries with it the risk of driving these businesses underground, thereby undermining our ultimate regulatory goals.

On balance, however, we believe that outlining the requirements for dealing with foreign agents and counterparties, including informal networks, is appropriate in light of the risks of money laundering and the financing of terrorism.

APPENDIX I – CHART OF RECORDKEEPING REQUIREMENTS

Recordkeeping Requirements			
31 CFR 103.29			
Entity	*Transaction Amount and Type*	*Authority and Record*	*Verification*
All Financial Institutions Requirements vary slightly depending on whether the purchaser has a deposit account	Issuance or sale of money orders, traveler's checks, or certain other negotiable instruments for $3,000 to $10,000 inclusive in currency	Purchaser's name, address, identification number, and date of birth Transaction date and type Serial number and amount of instruments	Verification of purchaser's name and address Record state of issuance and number of the person's driver's license or other document that was accepted for identification purposes Or, verification that the individual is a deposit account holder

Recordkeeping Requirements			
31 CFR 103.33			
Entity	*Transaction Amount and Type*	*Authority and Record*	*Verification*
Non-Bank Financial Institutions	Transmittals of funds (whether or not involving currency) of $3,000 or more	If sent, record: Transmitter's name, address, and Taxpayer Identification Number (TIN) Execution date, amount, instructions Identity of recipient's financial institution.	Verification of Transmitter's Name and Address Record of identification and the number of the identification document

Recordkeeping Requirements			
		If received, record: Recipient's name, address and specific identifier as well as "any form relating to the transmittal of funds that is completed or signed by the person placing the transmittal order" if the MSB is the sender. For recipients, the MSB is required to keep "The original or microfilm or other copy or electronic record of the transmittal order."	

Recordkeeping Requirements			
31 CFR 103.37			
Entity	*Transaction Amount and Type*	*Authority and Record*	*Verification*
Currency Dealers and Exchanges	When a transaction account is opened or a line of credit is extended, the dealer must record the taxpayer identification number. 31 CFR 103.37(a). There are numerous exemptions including governments, foreign diplomats, aliens temporarily in the United States (under 180 days or in college), and unincorporated tax exempt units that are covered by a group exemption letter. Under 31 CFR 103.37(b), the currency dealer or exchanger must also retain a record of: Bank statements, cancelled checks, etc. Daily work records needed to reconstruct currency transactions with customers and foreign banks	For each exchange of currency involving transactions in excess of $1,000: The customer's name and address, passport number or taxpayer identification number, date and amount of the transaction, and currency name, country, and total amount of each foreign currency	

Recordkeeping Requirements			
	Each exchange of currency involving transactions in excess of $1,000		
	Signature cards that must contain the name of the depositor, street address, and TIN as well as the signature		
	Each item greater than $10,000 remitted or transferred to a person, account, or place outside the United States		
	Each receipt of currency or other monetary instruments and of each transfer of funds or credit greater than $10,000 received not through a domestic financial institution from any person, account, or place outside the United States		
	Records made in the ordinary course of business needed to reconstruct an account and trace a check in excess of $100 through it to its depository institution		
	A record maintaining the name, address, and TIN of any person presenting a certificate of deposit for payment as well as a description of the instrument and date of transaction		
	A system of books and records that will enable the currency dealer to prepare an accurate balance sheet and income statement		

APPENDIX J – RECORDS COMMONLY FOUND AT MSBS

Examples of Records Commonly Found at Check Cashers

A check casher's records may include:

- Daily Cash Reconciliation (Log): a record summarizing the total currency transactions during the day that reconciles to the beginning and ending cash on hand;

- Teller Reconciliation: record detailing individual teller transactions, for both currency and monetary transactions. It reconciles beginning and ending cash on hand and is used to prepare the daily cash reconciliation;

- Daily Sales Sheet: a record of cash sales received from money order/traveler's check sales, funds transmittals, etc. and a record of cash disbursements including checks cashed, cash payrolls and other cash expenses;

- Canceled money orders/traveler's checks;

- Daily bank deposit slips;

- Bank statements;

- Signature cards;

- Transaction Account detailing an individual's record of checks cashed, including copies of checks cashed; and

- Monthly Bank Reconciliation: reconciles the bank accounts to the general ledger balances.

Records may be stored on microfilm, digital, scanned, and other electronic media.

- The check casher may retain microfilm, a copy, or a reproduction in lieu of the original document. The microfilm of checks cashed is often maintained instead of a check register; and

- An outside contractor often maintains offsite microfilm records. The examiner should ask the check casher to provide a written release to access the records.

If the records are maintained off site, the check casher must make the records accessible within a reasonable period of time, taking into consideration the nature of the records and the amount of time expired since each record was made. Use of a Computer Audit Specialist (if available) should be considered if records are voluminous.

Examples of Records Commonly Found at Currency Dealers or Exchangers:

A currency dealer's or exchanger's records may include:

- Daily cash drawer and vault reconciliations;

- Bank statements, deposit slips, and debit/credit memoranda; and,

- Funds transmittal confirmations;

- Customer records (either hard copy or electronic);

- Invoices and purchase orders;

- Annual Summary Sheet: a record of monthly transaction totals;

- Monthly Summary Sheet: a record of daily transaction totals for the month and the source document for preparing the annual summary sheet;

- Client Ledger Cards: a record of transactions with regular clients (larger currency dealers or exchangers may maintain this record);

- Daily Transactions Log: a record summarizing daily transactions. This is the source document for preparing the monthly summary sheet and includes the beginning and ending cash balances. If cash balances are not maintained on this record, a separate cash (vault) inventory record is usually maintained;

- Transaction Vouchers: a record of each transaction that shows the date, amount and rate of exchange. This record may, but usually does not, include customer identification for transactions over $1,000. This is the source document for preparing the daily transaction log;

- Domestic Bank Records: these should include all account statements, duplicate deposit tickets, canceled checks, funds transmittal confirmation statements, and other debit and credit memoranda; and

- Copies of CTRs and SAR-MSBs.

Other books and records may include a general ledger, receipt and disbursement journals, and invoices and receipts. Records may also include foreign bank account records and the records of domestic and foreign agents or nominees.

Examples of Records Commonly Found in Connection with Money Orders/Traveler's Checks

Money order agent records may include:

- Bank statements and deposit slips;
- Daily sales summaries;
- Customer records (electronic or hard copies);
- Carbons or duplicates of money orders/traveler's checks; and
- Commission statements.

Examples of Records Commonly Found at Money Transmitters

A money transmitter's records may include:

- Bank statements and deposit slips;
- The money transmitter's send and receive forms completed by the customers;
- Commission statements;
- Agent records of transactions of $3,000 or more; and
- Daily reconciliations and sales summary.